The Caregiver's Guide to Self-Care

Help for Your Caregiving Journey

By
Jane Meier Hamilton, MSN, RN

ISBN 978-0-7414-5802-5 Paperback
ISBN 978-0-7414-6881-9 eBook

Published by:

 **INFINITY** PUBLISHING

1094 New DeHaven Street, Suite 100
West Conshohocken, PA 19428-2713
Info@buybooksontheweb.com
www.buybooksontheweb.com
Toll-free (877) BUY-BOOK
Local Phone (610) 941-9999
Fax (610) 941-9959

Printed in the United States of America

Published September 2011

Contents

Preface

Your loved one needs your help and you are doing the very best you can. Some days helping feels like a privilege or joy. Thinking of how much they mean to you, how much they have given or how vulnerable they are, you throw yourself into caring. But at other times, caring for your loved one can be overwhelming and burdensome. So much of your own life is put on hold. So much of your energy and resources are spent. And your heart can be utterly broken by the pain and suffering you witness. If you withdraw or turn away, guilt rises; you wonder how you could react this way. But these mixed feelings are normal, human. Caring for another person is never easy. At times it is terribly difficult and painful. It can become unbearable. Being a caregiver can make you sick in body, mind and spirit. And this is why I wrote *The Caregiver's Guide to Self-Care: Help for Your Caregiving Journey.*

My caregiving journey spans the past thirty-five years. I have been a registered nurse and professional caregiver since 1973. But my family caregiving journey began twenty years ago with my husband who suffered nearly seven years of relentless pain while our son was a young child. Both my father and father-in-law battled lung cancer. Dad was legally blind in the last twenty years of his life. A major stroke disabled and finally took my mother-in-law. Other dear friends and family have died from Lou Gehrig's disease and various forms of cancer. It took Alzheimer's disease eight years to ravage and finally devour my sweet mother. That was the worst and last of my caregiving experiences. Mom died in September 2007. At the end of my family caregiving journey I was depleted, depressed and praying for release.

Since then I have recovered my energy, health and well-being. I have emerged from grief wiser, deeper, stronger. The losses have taught me lessons that I want to share with you. My caregiving experience has been the journey of a lifetime, uniquely mine, but so like others' experiences in many, many ways. One aspect of our caregiving experience is universal; all of us who give care need to take care. If we overlook our own needs, our physical and mental health suffers. We begin to feel alone, overwhelmed and unable to effectively help those in our care. I know. These things happened to me. I made some mistakes, but also did things that kept me going and sustained my capacity to care throughout all those years. These are the ideas that you will find within the seven chapters of this book.

This approach to self-care worked for me, and it is consistent with other research-based, stress-coping models for family caregivers. I call my model "the 7C's of self-care." In each chapter you will find:

- A brief story from my personal experience as a daughter grappling with my mother's Alzheimer's disease.
- Self-care recommendations from my professional experience as a psychiatric nurse that are based on research from the stress, caregiving and positive psychology literature.
- Self-care activities to help individual caregivers, groups of caregivers, or professionals who are helping caregivers. These are designed to guide you in applying self-care concepts in your life. Read through them all; focus on those that work for you.
- Caregiver resources that can help you find out more about self-care for caregivers.

Your loved one needs your help and you are doing the very best you can. What you are doing is so important, so rewarding, yet so challenging. Preserve your health, well-being and capacity to care. On your caregiving journey, care for yourself as you care for others. My earnest hope is that you find compassion, comfort and real help in *The Caregiver's Guide to Self-Care: Help for Your Caregiving Journey.* Thank you for allowing me to be among your partners on the path....

Jane Meier Hamilton, MSN, RN
November 2009

C1: Claim Your Caregiver Role

Jane's Story: There is a Season and a Time

I have been a caregiver many times during the past twenty years. Many members of my immediate and extended family have needed my help as they battled a host of serious illnesses. And I am not alone in this. Many of my close friends have cared for their spouses, parents and children, too. In some cases, those we love have died, but others now live with chronic conditions that have forever changed their lives. Seeing family and friends suffer has broken my heart and created within me a deep desire to help.

For me, the desire and ability to care for my loved ones was like a precious pearl, secreted away for safe keeping. Our bonds of affection created this pearl of great price. When their days of need arrived, I reached deep within to where the pearl was hidden. Out of love and compassion I redeemed that treasure and spent all its worth to provide for them. Because I have felt their love, I wanted to return it with helpful, caring acts. This is how I became a caregiver. The time of their need became my season of care.

To everything there is a season and a time to every purpose under heaven. Is this your season of care? Is this your time to help a loved one? Is it your purpose to be a caregiver? Many people don't think of themselves as caregivers. They say,

- "I am his wife, not a caregiver."
- "She's my mother; after all she's done for me, it's the least I can do."
- "I am just helping my friend; I want to be there for him."
- "I never thought of myself as a caregiver; I just do things for my Dad."
- "We're family; it's no big deal."

Sometimes it is a big deal, though, even with the desire and ability to care. Occasionally it is a debt or duty, not voluntarily chosen. Caring for a loved one is not the same as being a paid or professional caregiver. At its best, family caregiving is not employment; it is a testament and repayment of love. Are you a family caregiver? If you are, recognize the wonderful gifts you give. Claim your caregiver role.

Self-Care Recommendations

What do you mean by "caregiver"? 1*

Within our families, neighborhoods, faith communities, workplaces, health care practices and circles of friends, we know people of all ages who are caring for loved ones. Today, in any given year over 65 million people in the US provide care for a chronically ill, disabled or aged family member, or special needs child. Based on demographic trends, these numbers are sure to rise in the years ahead. Many of these 65 million people don't think of themselves as caregivers. They see themselves not heroes but as helpers who are looking to give back, not get recognition.

Professional caregivers are the paid workers or unpaid volunteers who work in health care organizations, faith-based, or community organizations. Family caregivers are unpaid individuals who take care of their family members, friends or neighbors. They provide many types of care: emotional support, physical care and help managing household or personal affairs. (For a complete list, see pages 124-125) The amount of time spent on caregiving can range from a few hours a week to round the clock responsibility. Family caregivers can be primary caregivers, the person actually delivering care, or secondary caregivers, the person acting as backup support to other family members or to professionals who provide direct care. Family caregivers may live with their care recipient or live separately; they may share the same home, live down the street or across the country. Those who live more than an hour's travel distance from a care receiver are called long-distance caregivers.

Based on these descriptions, you may recognize yourself, or someone you know, as a family caregiver. Like others, you may not usually think of yourself in these terms, even though you do provide much support for a loved one…it's just something you do! If you or someone you know is acting as a family caregiver, it is important to identify yourself as a caregiver with important needs. Why?
- Providing ongoing care and assistance can take a physical, financial, emotional and spiritual toll.
- It can strain your work life and family relations.

- Overlooking the impact of caregiving puts you at risk of feeling isolated, overwhelmed, and becoming ill.
- Support from others and your our own self-care can help you stay healthy and strong enough to do one of the most important things you will ever do in life…and that's good for both you and your loved one.

So, if you or someone you know is a family caregiver, review these materials. You may have few free moments if you currently are caring for a loved one, but you owe it to yourself to invest some time to find resources and people who can help you. You are not alone. The first steps to receiving the support you need are recognizing your role as caregiver, and the stress that often comes with it.

"Caregiving is universal. There are only four kinds of people in the world: those who have been caregivers, those who currently are caregivers, those who will be caregivers, and those who will need caregivers."

Rosalynn Carter
First Lady; founder of The Rosalynn Carter Institute

"To pity distress is but human; to relieve it is Godlike."

Horace Mann
The father of American education

Self-Care Activities

Self-Care Activity #1: Claim your family caregiver role *2

Question #1. Am I a caregiver?
You may not think of yourself as a caregiver; even though you do a lot to help your loved one...it's just something you do! Check the four ways that caregivers typically offer help to loved ones. If you assist in any of these ways, yes, you are a family caregiver.

Read the statements below. Circle the number that best describes your experience:	Constantly	Very often	With some regularity	Very rarely	Never
A. I provide physical care: feed, bathe, dress, groom, toilet, or help with walking.	4	3	2	1	0
B. I manage household affairs: cook, clean, shop, launder clothes, do home repairs, or help with relocation.	4	3	2	1	0
C. I manage personal affairs: medicine, finances, legal, insurance, care coordination, or transportation.	4	3	2	1	0
D. I provide emotional or social support: help with behavior, moods, socializing, or making decisions.	4	3	2	1	0
To tally your score, add the numbers circled in each column, and then add the numbers across this row. My total for Question #1 is:_____					

Interpreting My Score

Higher numbers suggest the need to focus on self-care because you may be vulnerable to the effects of caregiver stress. Any of these scores can change over time, so check yourself again in the future, as a way to keep aware of your situation.

Any total score above "4" indicates that you have taken on a family caregiving role. Thinking of yourself as a caregiver is important because it opens your eyes to the:

- Beautiful gift you give when helping others in need.
- Toll that caregiving can take on you.
- Need to protect your health, well-being and capacity to care.

Total scores of 1-7 suggest that you are not burdened by caregiving at this time. To stay strong and prevent problems, review action steps found in the chart on pages 16-17. Work on those for Caregiving Stages 2 and 3.

Total scores of 8-16 reveal that you have significant caregiving responsibilities. Though these may be very meaningful to you, they may erode your well-being and health, particularly if you have been a caregiver for a long time, or in difficult situations. Protect yourself. Select from ideas found in the action steps found in the chart on pages 16-17. Work on those for Caregiving Stages 3, 4 and 5.

Items with a score of 3 or 4 are areas where you are heavily involved. Regardless of your composite score, these responsibilities require energy and are demanding. Guard your well-being and capacity to care by using the healthy self-care practices outlined in the chart on pages 48-49.

Self-Care Activity #2: Are you ready? *3

Question #2. How ready am I to be a caregiver?
Like most people, you probably live a full and busy life. Helping your loved one is added to other priorities, relationships and responsibilities. Fitting this new role in with the rest of your life can be quite a challenge.

Read the statements below. Circle the number that accurately describes your experience:	Strongly agree	Agree	Neither agree nor disagree	Dis-agree	Strongly disagree
A. I am generally in good physical, mental, emotional and financial health.	0	1	2	3	4
B. I can comfortably balance caregiving responsibilities with work and family responsibilities.	0	1	2	3	4
C. I am willing to provide care and my loved one is willing to accept my care.	0	1	2	3	4
D. I generally have positive relationships with the care receiver and other family caregivers.	0	1	2	3	4
E. I know that I can get whatever help I need to give good care to my loved one.	0	1	2	3	4
To tally your score, add the numbers circled in each column, and then add the numbers across this row. My total for Question #2 is:_____					

Interpreting My Score

These items provide a snapshot of the context in which you help your loved one, how caregiving fits into your life.

Total scores of 0-5 signal strength and readiness to be a caregiver.

Total scores of 6-10, or responses of 2 to most items present no clear picture. Your strengths and resources may make up for some areas of vulnerability. You *may have some issues* that make caregiving a challenge: health, work-life balance, willingness, available resources or your relationship with your care receiver.

Total scores of 11-15 suggest that *helping your loved one can be challenging and can be uncomfortable* for you. Your own health, life responsibilities, relationships, or resources have some effect on your willingness and/or ability to care for your loved one.

Total scores of 16-20 show that *caregiving presents some significant challenges.* Your own health, life responsibilities, relationships and resources greatly impact your willingness and/or ability to care.

Higher numbers on this test suggest *you may be vulnerable* to the negative effects of caregiver stress. Nurture and sustain your strengths by regularly practicing self-care. Empower yourself by acknowledging your strong points reflected in items marked 0-2. Take action to improve any of the items marked 3 or 4. For detailed advice on self-care, read the text in the following chapters.

Any of your scores can change over time. Check yourself again in the future to remain aware of your situation.

Self-Care Activity #3:
What is the impact of caregiving? *4

Question #3. How am I being affected by being a caregiver?
Caring for a loved one can be both one of the most demanding and most fulfilling experiences you will ever have. Over time, caregiving can take a toll on your physical and emotional health, but it can offer benefits and blessings as well. Caring for a loved one affects different people in different ways.

Read the statements below. Circle the number that honestly describes your experience:	Strongly agree	Agree	Neither agree nor disagree	Dis-agree	Strongly disagree
A. Helping my loved one has caused disturbances in my physical or emotional health.	4	3	2	1	0
B. Being a caregiver has led to work-related or financial difficulties.	4	3	2	1	0
C. Caring for my loved one has led to isolation or difficulties with my family or friends.	4	3	2	1	0
D. I am pessimistic, uncomfortable, uncertain, or overwhelmed by caregiving responsibilities.	4	3	2	1	0
E. Helping my loved one has taken more satisfaction from my life than it has given me.	4	3	2	1	0
To tally your score, add the numbers circled in each column, and then add the numbers across this row. My total for Question #3 is:_____					

Interpreting My Score

These items provide a <u>snapshot of the consequences</u> of caregiving, how helping impacts your life.

<u>Total scores of 0-5</u> show that you feel able to handle your caregiving responsibilities.

<u>Total scores of 6-10</u> or <u>responses of 2 to most items</u> present no clear picture. Your strengths or positive outlook may make up for some of your vulnerabilities. *You may notice some subtle signs* from within you or from your work or personal life that signal caregiver stress.

<u>Total scores of 11-15</u> suggest that caregiving is *taking a toll in several areas of your life,* while other aspects are just fine. You see signs of stress in your health, work life, finances, family relationships, or outlook.

<u>Total scores of 16-20</u> indicate that your caregiving role is taking a toll on you and is having a *significant negative impact on your life.* Your own health, mental outlook, work life, finances, and/or family relationships are suffering.

<u>Higher numbers</u> on this test suggest loss of health and wellbeing that *signals vulnerability* to the negative effects of stress. Nurture and sustain your strengths by regularly practicing self-care. Empower and encourage yourself by acknowledging your strong points reflected in items marked 0-2. Take action to improve any of the items marked 3 or 4. For detailed advice on self-care read the text in the following chapters.

Any of your scores can change over time. Check yourself again in the future to remain aware of your situation.

Self-Care Activity #4:
Identify your place on the caregiving path *5

What stage of caregiving am I in?
As a caregiver, what you do and how you feel changes over time. Caregiving is a journey with a series of different stages along the way. Where are you on the caregiving path? Put a check mark on the line next to the stage that best describes you.

Stage 1: Preparing Myself

Approaching the path

Caring for my loved one is in my future.

Typical stage 1 experiences:

Observing growing needs in your loved one

Thinking they may soon need your help

<u>Feeling:</u> Surprise, concern about changes you see

<u>Wondering</u>: What lies ahead? Where can I turn for information?

Stage 2: Getting Started

Entering onto the path

I am starting to care for my loved one.

Typical stage 2 experiences:

Offering various types of help

Seeing how caregiving fits with your other roles

Learning about the condition, helpful resources

<u>Feeling:</u> Denial, fear, confusion, sadness, hopefulness

<u>Wondering:</u> What is happening? Why?

Stage 3: Actively Helping

Walking the path

I am offering care to my loved one.

Typical stage 3 experiences:

Helping regularly, for a number of months or years

Assuring your loved one's growing needs are met

Coordinating with others to offer help

<u>Feeling:</u> Ambivalence, satisfaction, frustration, fatigue, sadness

<u>Wondering:</u> What needs to be done? How will we do it?

Stage 4: Struggling Along

Staggering along the path

My caregiving continues and it's hard.

Typical stage 4 experiences:

Providing increasingly heavy level of care

Adjusting to your loved one's change/decline

Needing support to continue helping

Feeling: Resentment, guilt, anger, exhaustion, overwhelmed

Wondering: How long can this go on? How long can I go on?

Stage 5: Letting Go

Nearing the end of the path

Caregiving as I know it is ending.

Typical stage 5 experiences:

Preparing to change your role as caregiver

Facing loved one's end-of-life or "new normal"

Considering quality of life vs. longevity

Forgiving yourself and others

Feeling: Loss, release, powerlessness, introspective

Wondering: Is this really happening?

Stage 6: Moving On

Leaving the path

I am no longer a caregiver.

Typical stage 6 experiences:

Mourning

Reflecting on the lessons and meaning of caregiving

Sharing your wisdom

Considering your future

Feeling: Grief, pride, relief, regret, return of energy

Wondering: What does the future hold for me?

Self-Care Activity #5:
What are your caregiving priorities? *6

Based on what caregiving stage you are in, use the following chart to spell out your priorities, the work you need to do for your loved one, and for yourself.

Put a check mark on the line that best describes your situation.
Underline or highlight the tasks you need to do.

____	**Stage 1: Preparing Myself** My Priority: Get ready to help **Action steps for my loved one and myself:** Caregiving tasks: Gather information on health status of my loved one, their wishes about care, current health care providers, legal/financial/insurance issues, documents needed to manage their affairs Caring for myself: Obtain information about caregiving and caregiver stress
____	**Stage 2: Getting Started** My Priority: Take-up the caregiver role **Action steps for my loved one and myself:** Caregiving tasks: Develop a comfortable, effective routine; see what works Identify tasks I do/don't want to do, aspects of health care, skills for providing care, how to work with care receiver Develop skills, knowledge, competence Find help: Family/friends; support group; community organizations/faith communities Caring for myself: Recognize my caregiver role; find ways to calm myself; take breaks; identify sources of caregiver stress; develop caregiving skills; begin developing a network of support
____	**Stage 3: Actively Helping** My Priority: Pace myself **Action steps for my loved one and myself:** Caregiving tasks: Follow a routine that works Identify my caregiver concerns Solve problems I control Review plan for end-of-life issues, if appropriate to my loved one's condition Ask for and accept help and support of any kind from those who can truly help Caring for myself: Do healthy things to ease my stress; cultivate network of support; enjoy respite and time-off

Stage 4: Struggling Along
My Priority: Adapt and endure

Action steps for my loved one and myself:
Caregiving tasks: Adjust routine to reflect changes in functioning
Ask for and accept help and support of any kind

Caring for myself: Think optimistic thoughts; choose wisely; resolve
conflicts; rely on my community of support; balance involvement and
detachment; find ways to calm myself; do healthy things to ease my stress;
get relief through respite/time off

Stage 5: Letting Go
My Priority: Adjust to progression of my loved one's condition

Action steps for my loved one and myself:
Caregiving tasks: Change the routine as my loved one changes
Advocate for my loved one's changing needs
Face end-of-life issues and say good-bye to relationships, routines and
roles, or...
Return to health, or a "New Normal" and establish new routines of daily life

Caring for myself: Let go of what no longer works; use healthy stress
management

Stage 6: Moving On
My Priority: Release the caregiver role

Action steps for my loved one and myself:
Caregiving tasks: Reinvest energy into new interests; develop new patterns
Guide and help other caregivers

Caring for myself: Allow myself to grieve, share stories of caregiving
experiences
Recognize how I have grown and changed

Self-Care Activity #6:
Consider these questions in self-reflection or discussions

1. What are the good parts of caring for my loved one? What gives me a sense of joy or happiness? What makes me laugh? What is meaningful to me or to my loved one? What am I proudest of doing? What is important about my being a caregiver?

2. What are the most difficult parts of caring for my loved one? What brings me sorrow or pain? What is frustrating or annoying about this role? How do these difficulties, sorrows or frustrations affect me?

3. What lessons have I learned from being a caregiver? How have I grown or changed as a result of caring for my loved one? How does being a caregiver enrich my life?

4. How can I use what I have read in C1? With whom can I share what I have learned about caregiving?

C1 References

*1 Sources:

Family Caregiver Alliance: <u>caregiver.org</u>
National Alliance for Caregiving: <u>caregiving.org</u>
National Family Caregivers Association: <u>thefamilycaregiver.org</u>

*2 Adapted from:

Beth Witrogen McLeod, Editor. *And Thou Shalt Honor: The Caregiver's Companion.* Rodale Press. 2002. Pages 30-32.

Based on work of The Pennsylvania State University Gerontology Center. University Park, PA..

*3 and 4 Adapted from:

National Center on Caregiving, Family Caregiver Alliance. *Caregiver Assessment: Principles, Guidelines and Strategies for Change.* Volume 1; April 2006. <u>www.caregiver.org</u>

The University of Maine Center on Aging. Orno, Maine. *Maine Primary Partners in Caregiving (MPPC) Project.* <u>www.mainecenteronaging.org</u>

* 5 and 6 Adapted from:

Denise Brown. *The Caregiving Years: Six Stages to a Meaningful Journey.* <u>caregiving.com</u>

National Family Caregivers Association and National Alliance for Caregiving. *Stages of Caregiving.* <u>caregiving.com familycaregiving101.org/stages</u>

Carolyn McIntyre. *The Three Stages of Caregiving.* <u>strengthforcaring.com/manual/about-you-am-i-a-caregiver</u>

C1 Caregiver Resources

American Association of Retired Persons (AARP):
www.aarp.org has a caregiving section that discusses caregiving options and support, long-term care financing, help with home care, housing options, assistive devices, and caregiving for adult children. Click on "Life Answers" on the main page to access caregiving information.

And Thou Shalt Honor: www.andthoushalthonor.org is a website companion to the PBS special and text of the same name that is cited below.

Ask Medicare: www.medicare.gov/caregivers provides Medicare beneficiaries and their caregivers a wide range of consumer-friendly tools and materials designed to lighten the burden of caregiving and help make informed healthcare decisions.

Delehanty, Hugh and Ginzler, Elinor. *Caring for Your Parents: The Complete Family Guide.* AARP/Sterling. 2005.

Mace, Nancy and Rabins, Peter. *The 36 Hour Day: A Family Guide to Caring for Persons with Alzheimer's Disease, Related Dementing Illnesses and Memory Loss in Later Life. Revised Edition.* Grand Central. 2001.

McLeod, Beth Witrogen Editor. *And Thou Shalt Honor: The Caregiver's Companion.* Rodale, 2002.

National Family Caregivers Association (NFCA):
www.thefamilycaregiver.org is one of the most complete caregiving sites. It provides caregivers with tips on caregiving, advocacy updates, information on communicating effectively with

healthcare professionals, opportunities to share your caregiving story and much more. Call them at: 1-800-896-3650

Rhodes, Linda. *The Complete Idiot's Guide to Caring for Aging Parents.* Alpha Books. 2001.

❧

"It's only natural to feel overwhelmed by the prospect of adding caregiving to an already full plate. Ambivalence toward caregiving should be considered a normal, expectable reaction that doesn't invalidate your love or devotion to your ill family member."

Dr. Barry Jacobs
Psychologist; author of *The Emotional Survival Guide for Caregivers*

"What makes caregiving appear difficult is the inner journey, the one that requires us to summon the courage and flexibility to relate to life in an unfamiliar but more expansive way…Caregiving has heart and meaning because it changes us for the better."

Beth Witrogen McLeod
Writer, speaker and consultant on caregiving issues

C2: Consider The Facts About Caregiver Stress

Jane's Story: Lost in the Line of Duty

Just this morning, I had a startling realization: I am lost! I usually know where I am going, and I generally reach my goal. But for the first time, I see that I am lost, not in a geographical sense, but in other different and disturbing ways. I have lost my zest for life; my energy is low and I am grief-stricken about Mother's dementia. I have lost my confidence about the future; I have no idea where this disease will take Mom and the rest of us, too. I am often lost in thought, preoccupied with how to get everything done and keep all the balls in the air. I have lost important parts of my life: my image of my parents as strong, vibrant people; my illusions of immortality and invulnerability; my hope that good people will be spared suffering; my sense of being someone's child.

Parts of my life are dead and gone. My mind is confused and preoccupied. In giving of myself to help my parents, I have lost parts of myself. What are the costs of trading off parts of my life over an extended period of time? What are the benefits? What choices do I have? I am betting that I won't always be lost. I want to help because Mom and Dad won't always need me as they do now. I am gambling that important parts of me can be revived. I hope I am right.

Where are you on your caregiving journey?

When I wrote "Lost in the Line of Duty" I was just waking up to the fact that caring for my parents had become a chronic source of stress. It was beginning to take a toll and I was starting to see my need for help. What had begun as a natural desire to give something back to my parents had silently morphed. Unbeknownst to me, I had become a caregiver. I was beginning to notice other caregivers, many who were doing much, much more than I was. That gave me hope. If they could manage, so could I.

The people or diagnoses in your circumstances may be different than mine, but like me you are a caregiver. Where are you in the caregiving journey? Are you lost in the line of duty? What might be the costs and benefits of trading off parts of your life over an extended period of time? Though meaningful, caregiving is stressful and can take a toll on your physical and mental health. Explore the facts about caregiver stress found in C2 and the many self-care suggestions found throughout the 7C's. These ideas can strengthen you and help preserve your capacity to care.

Self-Care Recommendations

Why do I need to understand caregiver stress?

Though it can be deeply rewarding, giving care is not an easy job; over time, it can make you sick. Family caregivers face a litany of challenges: physical demands, financial pressures, emotional ups and downs, major changes in roles and responsibilities, unfamiliar patient care duties, and worries about a loved one's welfare, 24/7. When caregiving goes on for a long time, it erodes your immune system and increases your susceptibility to disease; it increases your risk for depression and hospitalization. It is no wonder that 20 to 30% of family caregivers suffer from psychological and mood disturbances. Caregivers use prescription drugs for depression, anxiety, and insomnia two to three times as often as the rest of the population. For your own health and quality of life, it is important that you understand and learn to handle caregiver stress.

What is caregiver stress?

Stress is how the body responds to any demand (Life's demands are called stressors.) Caregiver stress is how you respond to the demands of being a caregiver. Viewed positively, the demands of caregiving are rewarding or challenging, and actually give you positive energy, but when experienced as negative, caregiver stressors create wear and tear on your body, mind and spirit. Whether your perceptions are positive or negative, the stress response unfolds as a self-protective process of adaptation that safeguards you and keeps you alive. The nature of your adaptation changes during each phase of the stress response, diagrammed on the top of page 26. No matter how different, each phase of the stress response is protective.

Three Phases of the Stress Response

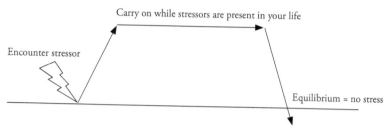

Carry on while stressors are present in your life

Encounter stressor

Equilibrium = no stress

Phase 1 Alarm
1. Encounter stressors
2. Fight/flight response:
   - Stressors = threats
   - Gear up to deal with stressors

Phase 2 Resistance
1. Endure stressors over time
2. Symptoms are warning signals:
   - Ignore symptoms & stress will worsen
   - Continued stress may endanger health
3. Can't resist stressors indefinitely

Phase 3 Exhaustion
1. Develop stress-related illnesses:
   - Force you out of action to repair body, mind and spirit
   - Illness creates more stress
2. Become unable to function

Caregiver stress, your health, and the quality and length of your life are all tied together, so it is very important to learn how to handle stress effectively. You have only one body and one life to live. In addition to interfering with your health, mismanaged stress also interferes with your work life, personal life and caregiving relationships. Using effective stress management techniques protects you from some of these negative effects of stress.

What are symptoms and sources of caregiver stress?

Recognizing stress in your life requires assessment of two key factors: the symptoms and the sources of stress. The symptoms of stress are a defensive early warning system. They are your body's way of signaling that you are endangering yourself by remaining in contact with stressors. Symptoms occur while you are in the resistance phase of stress. They foreshadow the illness or burnout that occurs during the exhaustion phase.

The symptoms of stress are grouped into six categories—physical, emotional, mental, social, occupational and spiritual. Everyone manifests symptoms of stress in each of these six categories, but because every human being is unique, each person experiences their own distinct set of symptoms. Use the Stress Symptoms Checklist found on pages 28-29 to identify which symptoms you experience.

Stressors are life's challenges and demands that cause stress. Some come from within you, while others come from your relationship with the environment and people around you. Internal stressors are the physical aspects of your own body, the emotions you experience or the demands which you place on yourself. External stressors arise from physical aspects of your environment—a wide range of factors like storms, traffic jams, power outages, crowded or dirty living arrangements. They also come from the needs, expectations and behaviors of other people. Every human being experiences a mix of internal and external stressors every day.

As a caregiver, you deal with an additional collection of stressors that arise from the responsibilities of helping your loved one. Some common caregiver stressors are listed in Self-Care Activity #2, found on pages 30-33. Use the three checklists in this activity to help you identify the sources of your caregiver stress. When you have completed the assessment of your symptoms (Self-Care Activity #1) and stressors (Self-Care Activity #2), proceed to C3, which will show you practical ways to care for yourself as you care for others.

Self-Care Activities

Self-Care Activity #1:
What are your symptoms of caregiver stress?

<u>Stress Symptoms Checklist</u>
It is important to be aware of stress symptoms; left unchecked, they lead to stress-related illnesses. Make a check on the line next to any of the caregiver stress symptoms you experience.

Physical

— Change in appetite   — Hyperventilation   — Restlessness
— Change in weight   — Trembling   — Chronic fatigue
— Eating junk food   — Muscle tension   — Insomnia
— Heavy drinking   — Teeth grinding   — Nightmares
— Smoking   — Nail biting   — Headache
— Drug abuse   — Clumsiness   — Sexual difficulties
— Stomach problems   — Stooped posture

Emotional

— Complaining   — Mood swings   — Vulnerability
— Crying   — Depression   — Fear
— Guilt or shame   — Apathy   — Frustration
— Irritability   — Inability to feel or   — Anger
— Mistrust   express emotions   — Loneliness
— Anxiety or panic   — Grief or loss

Mental

— Indecisiveness   — Wishing to return   — Boredom
— Difficulty   to life as it was   — Confusion
   concentrating   before caregiving   — Negativity
— Forgetfulness   — Diminished   — Denial
— Preoccupation   creativity

Social		

— Isolation
— Uncomfortable
  being alone
— Sullenness
— Defensiveness
— Blaming others
— Nastiness
	— Quarreling
	— Tension in
	  relationships
	— Dominating
	  conversations
	— Withdrawing from
	  conversations
		— Lack of pleasure
		  from experiences
		  you usually enjoy

Occupational

Caregiving work
— Overwhelmed
— Unprepared for tasks
— Turned off by distasteful tasks
— Difficulty making decisions/plans

— Feel no one understands
— Carrying caregiving
  burdens alone
— Conflict with other caregivers

Employment/home work
— Worry about work during
  "off" hours
— Coming to work late/leaving early
— Less energy for, or interest in work
— Being distracted

— Lower than normal
  quality or productivity
— Normal tasks are overwhelming
— Absenteeism
— Tardiness

Spiritual

— Doubt self-worth
— Seeing life as
  meaningless
— Hopelessness
	— Loss of faith or
	  ability to pray
	— Withdrawal from
	  faith community
		— Cynicism
		— Anger at God
		— Doubts about God
		— Asking, "Why me?"

Self-Care Activity #2: What causes your caregiver stress?

The demands that cause stress are called "stressors." Caregiver stress is caused by many different pressures that come from within you, from your job as a caregiver, and from the person who is receiving your care. Use the three checklists that follow to identify what causes your caregiver stress.

Make a check next to those items that apply to you on Stressor Checklist #1.

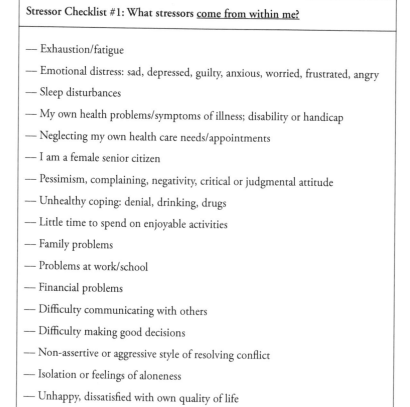

Stressor Checklist #1: What stressors <u>come from within me?</u>

— Exhaustion/fatigue

— Emotional distress: sad, depressed, guilty, anxious, worried, frustrated, angry

— Sleep disturbances

— My own health problems/symptoms of illness; disability or handicap

— Neglecting my own health care needs/appointments

— I am a female senior citizen

— Pessimism, complaining, negativity, critical or judgmental attitude

— Unhealthy coping: denial, drinking, drugs

— Little time to spend on enjoyable activities

— Family problems

— Problems at work/school

— Financial problems

— Difficulty communicating with others

— Difficulty making good decisions

— Non-assertive or aggressive style of resolving conflict

— Isolation or feelings of aloneness

— Unhappy, dissatisfied with own quality of life

To tally your score, add up the number of checks you made.
— **My Total** for Stressor Checklist #1 There are 17 items on this list.

Self-Care Activity #2:
What causes your caregiver stress? (Continued)

Continue this activity by checking the items that apply to you on Stressor Checklist #2.

Stressor Checklist #2: What stressors <u>come from my work as a caregiver?</u>

— My lack of knowledge: Loved one's condition or caregiving responsibilities

My lack of skill or confidence; discomfort/difficulties in:

   — Providing physical care

   — Managing household affairs

   — Managing personal affairs

   — Providing emotional or social support

— Reluctance to give care, or no choice about being a caregiver

— Witnessing pain or suffering of my loved one

— Unable to make things better for my loved one; no control

— Overinvolvement in, or disengagement from caregiving duties

— Overwhelming responsibility: Caring 24/7 or for a long time; helping with personal care more than 20 hours/week

— Always need to be on guard about my loved one's safety

— Difficulties with professional or paid care providers

— Difficulties with other family caregivers or my care receiver

— Expecting perfection of myself or others

— Others' expectations of me as a caregiver

— Unaware of where to get help

— Little or no respite from caregiving responsibilities

— Unreliable/no network of support: family, friends, neighbors, community resources, faith or workplace community

— Unable to afford to purchase necessary equipment, supplies or services

---

    To tally your score, add up the number of checks you made.
— **My Total** for Stressor Checklist #2. There are 19 items on this list.

Self-Care Activity #2:
What causes your caregiver stress? (Continued)

Complete this activity by checking the items that apply to you on Stressor Checklist #3.

Stressor Checklist #3: What stressors <u>come from my care receiver?</u>

— Long-term illness/disability

— Complex or high-intensity needs

— Unclear health status or priorities for care

— Worsening condition

— Physical, emotional or spiritual signs of suffering

Can't function independently/ heavy dependence on me for:

— Providing physical care

— Managing household affairs

— Managing personal affairs

— Providing emotional or social support

— Problems with thinking; dementia

— Poor insurance benefits

— Poor relationship with me and other caregivers

— Nasty, difficult or unpleasant behavior

— Pessimism, complaining, negativity, critical or judgmental attitude

— Emotional turmoil: sad, depressed, guilty, anxious, worried, frustrated, angry

— Unwilling to accept condition

— Ungrateful, unwilling to accept help

— Unhealthy coping behaviors: denial, drinking, drugs

— Married to, or living in same household with me

To tally your score, add up the number of checks you made.
— **My Total** for Stressor Checklist #3. There are 19 items on this list.

Interpreting My Score

The items in these three checklists provide detailed information about what causes you caregiver stress.

There are a total of 55 items.

The higher the total numbers of stressors you identified, the greater likelihood that you are, or will be experiencing some difficulties with caregiving.

Higher scores put you at risk for developing stress related illnesses that could undermine your ability to perform your important caregiver role. Be careful. Protect yourself and your loved one who depends on you for assistance. Use the healthy self-care practices described in the remaining chapters of this book.

Self-Care Activity #3:
Consider these questions in self-reflection or discussions

1. Has being a caregiver caused me to lose parts of myself or my life? If so, what have I lost? What are the costs of letting these things go? What are the benefits? What has this experience been like?

2. What symptoms of stress do I most commonly experience? What symptoms do I observe in my caregiving partners? What symptoms do I see in the one for whom I am caring?

3. How do I typically respond to stress symptoms: my own and those of others? Do I ignore them and keep going or heed their warning and do something to care for myself? What is the impact of my typical response? What things could I do to respond in a healthier way?

4. Have I developed stress-related illnesses as a result of being a caregiver? If so, what are they and what am I doing to take care of myself? What more could I do?

5. What are the main causes of my caregiver stress? Do they mostly come from within, from the work of caregiving, or from my care receiver? Have there been any changes in my stressors? What caused these to change?

6. Which stressors bother me most, and why is this so? What am I doing that helps me cope with these stressors? Is it working? Is there something more I could do?

C2 Caregiver Resources

Abramson, Alexis. *The Caregiver's Survival Handbook*. Perigee, 2004.

Davis, Martha et.al. *The Relaxation & Stress Reduction Workbook. 6th edition*. New Harbinger. 2008.

Loverde, Joy. *The Complete Eldercare Planner. 2nd edition*. Three Rivers Press. 2000.

Strength for Caring: www.strengthforcaring.com is an online resource and community for family caregivers as part of The Caregiver Initiative, created by Johnson & Johnson Consumer Products.

Zukerman, Rachelle. *Eldercare for Dummies*. Wiley. 2003.

"One critical step to easing the stress—and guilt—of caregiving is to admit that you can't do it alone and to seek help. Many caregivers rely on a combination of family and paid help."

Alexis Abramson
Author of *The Caregiver's Survival Handbook*

"The greatest weapon against stress is our ability to choose one thought over the other."

William James
American philosopher and psychologist

C3: Care For Yourself As You Care For Others

Jane's Story: Support Group

You want me to do what!? Attend a support group? Yeah, right! I could fit that in after my ten-hour day at work, just before I stop to buy the Depends for my mom, on the way to pick up the kids from practice and go home to make dinner. Or, maybe after dinner, when the dishes are cleared and I've finally managed to get the kids off the computer and phone and on to their homework. Or, perhaps between doing loads of laundry and calling my brothers to remind them that Mom is doing OK, but would really like to see them. You want me to take time for myself!? I don't see how I could possibly add one more thing to my plate, even if it is something good for me. It would just stress me out more to try to make the arrangements.

Sometimes words like these form in my mind, or actually come out of my mouth when others suggest I take a break from the rigors of caregiving. I dismiss others' suggestions for self-care. Why do I do this? Am I in such a rut that I can't see even just a few ways to reprioritize, reorganize, or reschedule parts of life so I can grab some time for me? Am I feeling so unworthy that I believe everyone else's needs really are more important than mine?

Am I feeling so guilty to be healthy when Mom is suffering, that I won't allow myself to stop; so blind to the consequences of living an overextended life that I can't see the real possibility of becoming sick from too much stress?

Whatever the reasons, taking some kind of self-care action now is more important than understanding why I haven't until now. What I need is some respite, a break that will help me relax and regain some energy. Maybe finding time to go out to a support group is beyond what I can do today. But I know there are lots of other things that can relieve my stress and give me strength for the journey ahead. I just need to do some of them.

How are you caring for yourself?

I went through a period during my caregiving years when I was always sick, nothing really serious but mostly annoying and inconvenient. A series of sinus infections plagued me for years. On the plane ride home from one trip to see my mom, I contracted a nasty virus which was not diagnosed for three months, and which kept me sick and tired for another three months. I was depressed and my immune system was shot. I spent more days in bed that winter than I had since infancy! Feeling lucky that it was nothing more serious, I realized that caregiving had silently stolen my vitality. How are you? Are you experiencing any signs of strain? What have you done for yourself lately? If you need to take better care of yourself, here are a few ideas that might be useful.

Self-Care Recommendations

What is self-care and why is it important?

Relief from the stress of caregiving starts with recognizing the importance of self-care and practicing it regularly. What is self-care? Self-care is being concerned about yourself, as well as others; looking out for your own welfare, making sure that your needs are met, not only those of others. Self-care is that collection of choices you make and behaviors you practice that make you feel good, solve your problems and ultimately, relieve your stress. Managing stress by practicing self-care is important because it protects your health, helps you cope when the things that cause stress are beyond your control, and helps you maintain the balance you require to care in a loving and effective way.

How can I practice self-care?

1: Name your symptoms and sources of stress

All successful self-care follows from this first step. Use the four checklists found in C2, on pages 28-32. for detailed descriptions that will help you name your symptoms and sources of caregiver stress.

2: Adjust your attitude

You can control the wear and tear of distress you experience by adjusting your attitude in the following ways:

- Positive self-talk: Silently or aloud affirm your strength and ability to cope. Think, "I can do this!"
- Challenging negative beliefs: Question negative assump-

tions. Consider possible positive outcomes. Ask yourself, "What is the worst that could happen? What is the best that could happen? What is most likely to happen?"

- Relabeling: Think and talk about stress from a positive, not a negative perspective. Replace, "This is an awful problem." Instead think, "This is a challenge or opportunity."

3: Decide on a course of action

Ask yourself: **Is there anything I can do to change or eliminate the stressors in my life?** A yes or no answer leads to different approaches to self-care. Here are two examples.

Imagine your stressor is a disagreement with others over division of caregiving tasks. You are tired, have other pressing responsibilities and need some help. In this case your answer to the question would be, "Yes. If I take some action the stressor could be relieved, or will completely go away. My friends or family may help me if I ask them." When you control or can influence stressors, the best course of action is assertiveness and problem solving. This approach will yield relief and may even eliminate your stressors. Be sure to use a positive approach when solving problems.

In a second scenario, the stressor is your loved one's Alzheimer's disease, the progression of their illness and the suffering that goes with it. Here your answer to the question would be, "No. No matter what I do the diagnosis won't change or go away. I need to find some way to live with this." When you have no control or influence over your stressor, the best course of action is using healthy self-care practices. Problem solving or assertiveness won't have an effect. Self-care helps you retain energy and feel better when stressors are beyond your control.

One caution: Take care that you don't reply "no" to the question of your ability to change or eliminate stress when, with courage, you could answer "yes." Check your perceptions with a reliable person.

4: Use healthy self-care practices daily, as well as when you lack control

Loss of control is very stressful. When there is nothing to be done, the thing to do is to care for yourself.

And don't wait until you have already worn down to practice self-care; make it a priority in your daily routine. Choose things that are good for your body, heart, mind and spirit. Some are self-soothing—whatever helps you calm down, have fun, relax, enjoy or feel pampered. Others involve self-discipline; although less pleasurable, in the long run, disciplined self-care practices lead to a greater sense of well-being. See Self-Care Activity #2 found on pages 48-49 for examples of healthy self-care.

5: Use problem-solving skills when you have control

When some action on your part can ease or eliminate your stress, take problem-solving action by using the four-step process outlined below.

Step 1: Figure out what your problem is:

Name the challenge, opportunity, difficulty, or situation that needs improvement. If emotions or confusion makes this difficult, ask those you respect and trust for help. Organize your facts:

- WHO contributed to this problem? WHO was affected?
- WHAT happened to create this problem: violated expectations or promises, bad behavior, something else?
- WHEN did this happen?

- WHERE did this happen?
- HOW do you and others feel in response to this problem?
- WHY is this important?

Step 2: Develop a problem-solving plan.

- Consider options. Ask: What can be done to resolve this problem? Brainstorm to develop possible solutions; the more options you create, the more likely you will identify an effective solution.
- State desired outcomes. Ask: What do I want to achieve? What are short and long-term goals? What rewards will I get if this problem is solved?
- Write an action plan. Create a three-column chart with these headings, like the one found in Self-Care Activity #3 on page 50. Fill in the details.

  1. WHAT: Name each step and the tasks for accomplishing it. Think about what difficulties might arise and how you could handle them.

  2. WHO: Name the person(s) who will be responsible for doing each step of the plan.

  3. WHEN: Identify deadlines for completing each task.

Step 3: Carry-out your plan.

Take action and check for progress. Tracking progress is critical; it motivates people to follow through on the plan. Remind those involved of deadlines for each step and for the whole plan, the desired outcomes, and rewards for success.

Step 4: Evaluate your plan.

Ask: Did we solve the problem? Did we achieve our goal? Did we change the situation? Are we listening to all feedback, both positive and critical? Does anything more need to be done? What have we learned from this situation? What worked? What didn't work?

6: Avoid stress-numbing behaviors

Stress-numbing behaviors include: complaining and blaming; drugs and drinking; over eating and consuming junk food; buying sprees; smoking; sleeping to avoid stress; burying yourself in television, video games, the computer or other distractions; or avoiding action on problem-solving. These behaviors numb the distress of being a caregiver, but do nothing to help body, mind or spirit cope in a healthy way with caregiving challenges. By promoting a sense of release or relaxation, they give the illusion of self-care, but if overused, or used in place of problem-solving action, can actually create more stress than they relieve.

What stress-numbing behaviors do you use? How much do you rely on them to dull the pain or discomfort in your life? Make sure that these are not big parts of your approach to self-care. If you are too reliant on any of these practices, look for alternatives that are healthier and more effective.

"The biggest complaint among caregivers is lack of personal time. Make some. Your own good health and happiness are gifts to your loved ones."

Suzanne Mintz
Founder: National Family Caregivers Association

Self-Care Activities

Self-Care Activity #1:
Consider these questions in self-reflection or discussions

1. What are the major symptoms that show I am experiencing caregiver stress? (Return to the Stress Symptoms Checklist found on pages 28-29. Use it to help you answer this question.)

2. What causes my caregiver stress? (Return to the three stressor checklists found on pages 30-32. Use them to help you answer this question.)

3. If I adjust my attitude, would that help relieve some of my stress? If so, what are the negative thoughts I should let go and what positive thoughts should replace them?

4. What stress-numbing behaviors do I turn to for relief? Am I overly reliant on these? What healthier practices could replace some of my current stress-numbing behaviors?

5. What healthy self-care practices have already helped me handle stressors that are beyond my control? Are there any new behaviors or practices that I could add: things that are soothing, fun, energizing, relaxing, or feel like a treat?

6. What one or two things will I do to care for myself today?

Self-Care Activity #2:
What healthy self-care practices do you currently use?

Healthy Self-Care Practices

Assess how well you take care of yourself by checking each self-care practice you currently use.

Physical

- Exercise
- Rest during the day
- Sleep 8 hours at night
- Eat a balanced diet
- Limit "junk food"
- Drink eight glasses of water daily
- Maintain weight in desired range
- Limit alcohol consumption
- Do not smoke
- Get regular checkups
- Use medications as prescribed
- Practice the relaxation response
- Groom yourself-manicure, facial, haircut, shave, etc.
- Get a massage

Emotional

- Allow yourself to feel emotions
- Express emotions appropriately and respectfully
- Resolve conflicts
- Nurture yourself
- Don't take things too seriously
- Work off anger with physical exercise
- Say "no" when you want or need to
- Ask directly for what you want
- Cry
- Laugh

Mental

- Ask questions
- Accept ambiguity
- Read
- Take risks
- Daydream
- Learn something new
- Consider different viewpoints
- Relabel unpleasant situations
- Develop plans
- Think optimistically

Social

- Develop and use support systems
- Talk with friends and family
- Take time off
- Go on vacation
- Rehabilitate or end unsatisfactory relationships
- Limited TV viewing
- Engage in a creative pastime or hobby
- Socialize with others
- Enjoy intimacy or sex
- Play
- Spend time alone
- Treat yourself to something that you enjoy-new clothes, CD, magazine, etc.

Occupational		
Caregiving work		
— Learn new skills	— Share responsibilities	
— Pace yourself	— Let others do a stressful task	
— Balance involvement and detachment	— Beautify your environment	
— Seek respite-daily, periodic, short term, vacations	— Acknowledge the good you do	
Employment/home work		
— Get organized	— Leave work at work	
— Take breaks	— Develop good relationships with co-workers	
— Pace yourself	— Open yourself to change	
— Do your best and let the rest go		

Spiritual		
— Pray	— Attend worship services	— Take one day at a time
— Meditate	— Read inspirational prose or poetry	— Clarify your values and beliefs
— "Let go" of unsolvable problems	— Appreciate the beauty of art and music	— Acknowledge your self-worth
— Commune with nature		

Interpreting My Score

A short list of checked items or one that has no checks in several sections indicates that you are not attending to your needs. You may be at risk for developing stress-related illnesses. A long and diverse list of self-care practices is a sign that you know how to take care of yourself. Be sure that you regularly use these practices or you may also be at risk. Re-read item #4 on page 42 of this chapter. It gives you the rules of thumb for practicing healthy self-care.

Self-Care Activity #3:

If you have a problem, how can you solve it?

Refer back to the four-step problem-solving process, described in Item #5 on pages 42-44. Use these steps to help you outline how you will solve a specific caregiving problem you are currently facing. Seek ideas from others to help you choose your best course of action.

Step 1: <u>My problem</u> is:

Step 2: <u>My action plan</u> will be specific and describe these three things: (Use another paper if you need more space.)

WHAT: Name each step or task for accomplishing the outcomes I desire.	WHO: Person(s) responsible for this step or task.	WHEN: Identify deadlines for completing each step or task.

Step 2 (continued): <u>My action plan</u> will achieve these desired outcomes:

Step 3: I will <u>carry-out my plan</u> and check progress in these ways:

Step 4: I will <u>evaluate my plan</u> by answering these questions:

- Did we solve the problem?

- Did we achieve our goal?

- Did we change the situation?

- Are we listening to all feedback, both positive and critical?

- Does anything more need to be done?

- What have we learned from this situation?

- What worked? What didn't work?

C3 Caregiver Resources

Barg, Gary. *The Fearless Caregiver.* Capital Books. 2003.

Berman, Claire. *Caring for Yourself while Caring for Your Aging Parents.* 2nd Edition. Henry Holt. 2001.

Caregiver: www.caregiver.com includes topic-specific newsletters, chat rooms, an online store and a free subscription to the online magazine, *Today's Caregiver.*

CarePages: www.carepages.com offers a free, secure website that connects friends and family during a health challenge. Support to caregivers is expanded with information, links and patient blogs.

Caring Bridge: www.caringbridge.org provides free, personalized patient information websites that connect family and friends during serious health events.

Jacobs, Barry. *The Emotional Survival Guide for Caregivers.* The Guilford Press. 2006.

Lotsa Helping Hands: www.lotsahelpinghands.com offers a free, private web-site that you can use to organize family, friends, neighbors, and colleagues during times of need. It allows you to easily coordinate activities and manage volunteers with an intuitive group calendar. You can also communicate and share information using announcements, messages boards and photos.

National Caregivers Library: www.caregiverslibrary.org has an extensive online library with hundreds of articles for caregivers, links to local resources and caregiver tools.

Strength for Caring: www.strengthforcaring.com Strength for Caring is an online resource and community for family caregivers as part of The Caregiver Initiative, created by Johnson & Johnson Consumer Products

"To keep the body in good health is a duty...otherwise we will not be able to keep our mind strong and clear."

Buddah
Philosopher, teacher, founder of Buddhism

"Forget the times of your distress, but never forget what they taught you."

Robert C. Gallagher
Author

"To give good care to others, we first must take care of ourselves. We can become handicapped as caregivers not because we lack knowledge about durable powers of attorney or long-term care insurance...but because we exclude ourselves from the care equation."

Beth Witrogen McLeod
Writer, speaker and consultant on caregiving issues

C4: Center Yourself

Jane's Story: What am I made of?

I feel really worn down and blue today. Caring for Mom and Dad is both a joy and a burden; deeply inspiring and repetitiously boring. It fills my heart and drains the last drop of energy I have; makes me proud of what I can do for my parents, yet guilty about how mad I get having to do it. For twenty years I have cared for different people in my family. Right now I am at a low point; caregiving is an arduous journey. My sister, Wendy, just sent me an email, one of those stories that circulate on the web, author unknown. Somehow, this anonymous little tale really speaks to me, as if Wendy wrote it just for me. The story from the web is titled *Carrots, Eggs or Coffee?* It goes like this:

A young woman went to talk with her mother and share how hard her life was. She did not know how she was going to make it and wanted to give up; she was tired of struggling. It seemed as if when one problem was solved, a new one arose.

The girl's mother took her to the kitchen. She filled three pots with water, and put them on the stove to boil. In the first, she placed carrots. In the second she placed eggs, and in the last pot, she placed ground coffee beans. The mother let them sit and boil without saying a word.

After twenty minutes, Mom turned off the burners, fished out the carrots and placed them in a bowl, removed the eggs from the second pot, and poured the steaming, aromatic coffee into a large mug. Turning to her daughter, the mother asked, "What do you see?" "Carrots, eggs and coffee," the young woman replied, wondering where this was going. The mother asked her daughter to feel the carrots, peel the hard boiled egg, and sip the cup of coffee.

Finally revealing the meaning of this odd exercise, the mother explained that each of these objects had faced the same "adversity," boiling water, but each had reacted differently. The carrot went in strong, firm, and unrelenting. However, after being subjected to boiling water, it softened and became weak. The egg had been fragile, with a thin outer shell protecting its fluid interior. Like the carrots, the egg was changed by the boiling water. Its soft interior became hardened. The mother pointed out that the coffee was unique; it alone had changed the water in which it had been boiled and turned it into something quite wonderful. Then she asked her troubled daughter, "Which one are you? In the face of adversity will you wilt and go soft, like the carrot? Will your fluid spirit harden, or, like the coffee beans, will you release the potential within you and turn the boiling waters of your life into something you savor?"

What are you made of?
Faced with adversity, what are you like: the carrot, eggs or coffee? Do you have the energy, judgment and grace to persevere

with caregiving? By centering yourself, you can tap into the wisdom and calm at your core and be like the coffee. Here are some ideas about how to do that.

Self-Care Recommendations

I am so overloaded! Why should I take the time for centering?

Would you like to handle caregiving with internal peace, balance and focused energy? These characteristics are always present deep inside you, no matter what intense emotions or anxious worries are churning within, no matter how tumultuous external events may be. They are always available if you are willing to reach for them, and if you develop the ability to connect with them through the practice of centering.

What can I do to feel more centered in my caregiving?

1. <u>Recognize the source of your energy</u>. As a human being, your life energy flows from living in harmony and balance, staying in tune with three factors:

    •Universal principles: Do unto others as you would have them do unto you. To everything there is a season. Honor your father and your mother. As you sow, so shall you reap. No man is an island. Violating universal principles like these creates disharmony and drains you. Follow universal principles.

    •Your human nature: You are physical, emotional, mental, social, and spiritual. Your personal energy flows when these five elements balance with the sixth element, the work that you do. Caring for all parts of yourself fills you with positive energy and helps you retain balance. Nurture all parts of yourself.

- **Your unique identity:** What distinguishes you from others? You have strengths and weaknesses; personal skills, qualities and a ways of doing things; values and principles that help you handle life challenges. Your life is richer and more satisfying when you know and respect your uniqueness. Be true to yourself.

2. <u>Understand how your energy flows.</u> You are human, not a machine. You are alive, operating on natural, not mechanical energy. You don't plug yourself in each morning and operate continuously like your computer or radio. You have cycles, with ups and downs. Like hours in a day or seasons in a year, your energy ebbs and flows. Your energy is affected by your environment. What goes on around you feeds or drains you, unlike machines that operate the same, whether the room is bright or dark. Accept and work with the natural flow of your energy so you can continue helping the ones you love.

3. <u>Balance involvement and detachment.</u> Balancing is the dynamic process of adapting to changing or competing demands. It involves consciously choosing what you will and won't do, based on what you can and can't handle. Balancing helps you avoid both dysfunctional over-involvement and distant disengagement from your caregiving role. Neither is healthy for you, your care receiver or other caregivers working with you. Be realistic about your limits; live within them to remain in balance. Say "No" to activities that draw you beyond what is reasonable for you to manage. Find alterna-

tive ways to deal with what you are unable to handle. Make readjustments to recover balance if you have become over-involved or disengaged from your caregiving role.

4. **Acknowledge your pain.** Bound together by the ties of family or friendship, you are affected by your loved one's condition. Though separate bodies, you are connected in your hearts and souls. Both of you grapple with intangible yet real heartaches that can take the form of distressing thoughts, feelings or physical symptoms. Borne alone, heartache slowly but inevitably erodes energy, health and peace of mind. Acknowledging your pain and sharing it with a trusted friend, counselor, member of your family or the clergy can help you. Open up and talk about your feelings.

5. **Conserve your energy.** Your energy is finite. Conserving your energy involves wise choices that must be made daily. Not always easy to make, they involve saying "no" to habits that waste time and energy.

    - **Define important.** Save your energy for what is important, not just what seems urgent.
    - **Eliminate the unimportant.** You can't do everything. Trim away non-essentials, others' priorities, busy-work or trivial activities that that do not reflect your values or help accomplish your goals.
    - **Sequence activities.** For activities that you do not want to eliminate, think about sequencing. Break large projects into parts and work on them step-by-step. Postpone what could be done later.
    - **Simplify your life.** Pare down what is complex or elabo-

rate so you can still enjoy favorite activities. Say "no" to overloading your schedule."

- **Avoid toxicity.** Stay away from people or situations that drag you down, erode your confidence or threaten your safety. If you must get involved with toxicity, protect yourself. Plan ahead what you will say or do. Ask supportive others to help you handle the negativity.

- **Let go of what you do not control.** However hard you try, well you plan, or carefully you communicate, you control very little of the total caregiving situation. Accept the limits of your humanity.

6. <u>Replenish your energy.</u> Use these four simple, but powerful techniques to center yourself and reenergize.

- **Breathe like a baby** Deep breathing lowers your heart rate, anxiety and muscle tension. It is the easiest way to elicit the relaxation response. In moments of high stress, pay attention to your breathing; breathe slowly and deeply from your abdomen. For the on-going stress of caregiving, make it a practice to breathe slowly and deeply for at least three minutes every day.

- **Clear your mind.** Worry, uncertainty and anxiety are frequent partners on the path of caregiving. They can escalate into catastrophic thinking that makes life miserable, wastes time, and interferes with effective problem-solving. Methods for clearing your mind include silence, prayer, journal writing, art, solitude, or communing with nature. Meditation is particularly effective. Practiced the world over in both the religious and non-religious context, meditation is intentionally and uncritically focusing attention on only one thing at a time. Meditating works because it is impossible for your body to simultaneously be relaxed and be in a state of stress.

- **Pursue your dreams.** Caring for your loved one isn't an either/or proposition; either your loved one's needs are met or yours are. It is more a question of finding ways to take good care of both your loved one and yourself. Pursuing what gives you joy and satisfaction, if only on a small scale, keeps the spark in your life and supplies energy to continue caring, however long and hard the journey. You experience a sense of calm when doing what makes you happy, not just what you think you should be doing. Take care not to put your dreams on hold.

- **Borrow from others.** The surest way to protect your health and restore depleted energy is to borrow some from your network. Reach out to anyone you know who could help: friends and family, people in your faith community or neighborhood, volunteers from community organizations, professional contacts, and people you could hire. If you are isolated or over-whelmed, change how you do what you do. Ask for help with caregiving work. Or seek help with managing aspects of your own affairs that are hard to get to because of caregiving responsibilities.

One last thought...

Centering yourself as a caregiver is like preparing to climb a tall mountain. You can not reach the summit without strength and stamina. Building–up your capacity to meet the challenges of an arduous journey is hard work. It takes commitment, wisdom, practice and patience. Persevering until you reach your goal demands regular refueling and periods of rest along the way. In caregiving, your ability to meet the challenge starts with an awareness of your needs and a commitment to caring in a balanced way. Start small, take your time, pace yourself and refuel regularly. With consistent focus on centering, you will develop the physical, emotional, and spiritual capacity to care...however long or demanding your journey.

"Don't neglect your own needs. Remember those airplane safety movies that instruct you to put your own oxygen mask on first, before assisting a child or someone who needs help? The logic is that you won't be much help to anyone if you are disoriented or passed out yourself."

Sasha Carr and Sandra Choron
Co-authors of *The Caregiver's Essential Handbook*

Self-Care Activities

Self-Care Activity #1:
Consider these questions in self-reflection or discussions

1. What is important to me about helping? What about it gives me joy, meaning, and pleasure? Which of my values and beliefs give me strength to do this work?

2. What are the gifts and talents I bring to being a caregiver? Who helps me with being a caregiver? What are the gifts and talents they contribute to caring for our loved one?

3. Do I feel overextended, off-balance, or low on energy? If so, what led me feel this way? What healthy ways of coping have helped me when I felt this way in the past? What would be helpful to me now?

4. How are my feelings of imbalance affecting my work: either caregiving or my occupation? How do any feelings of imbalance affect my health or relationships?

5. What/who feeds my positive energy and balance, my confidence or ability to give? Who could I ask to help me with any current loss of positive energy or confidence? How will I seek the help I need?

6. When I feel the loneliness, heartache or pain of being a caregiver, with whom can I share these feelings? Do I acknowledge this pain to myself or others? What are some healthy ways for me to handle the painful aspects of being a caregiver?

7. Am I putting my dreams on hold while being a caregiver? What could I do to continue feeling the joy and positive energy that come from pursuing my dreams, even if on a small scale?

8. What could I do to conserve my energy, and have more positive energy when caring for my loved one?

   a. What is unimportant that I could completely eliminate from my "to do" list?

   b. For things I don't want to eliminate, what could I postpone, or work on in small parts over time?

   c. What favorite activity/event could I pare down or do in a simpler way?

   d. What could I do to steer clear of the toxic people/situations that drain my energy or confidence? If I can't totally avoid these, what could I do to protect myself or limit the impact of these toxic people/situations?

Self-care activity #2:
How balanced is your involvement in caregiving? *1

Balancing helps you adapt to life's changing or competing demands. It helps you avoid both dysfunctional over-involvement and distant disengagement from your caregiver role. Neither is healthy for you, your care receiver or other caregivers working with you.

Read through the seven descriptions. Check the number that best describes your approach to caregiving.

——	**1. Detached:** You demonstrate no concern for the physical or emotional well-being of your loved one. You are disinterested and/or uninvolved in providing any type of care.
——	**2. Distant:** With prompting from others, you experience some concern about the well-being of your loved one. You are uninvolved in providing any type of care.
——	**3. Supportive:** You are concerned about the physical well-being of your loved one. You provide appropriate personal care freely and respectfully, but you maintain an emotional distance, as a professional would.
——	**4. Warmly supportive:** You are concerned about the physical as well as the emotional well-being of your loved one. You provide appropriate personal care freely and respectfully, with compassion and love.
——	**5. Occasionally over-involved:** You are warmly supportive of your loved one. Occasionally you sacrifice important parts of your own life, or take over certain aspects of your loved one's life that they, or others, could manage.
——	**6. Often over-involved:** You are warmly supportive of your loved one, but view caregiving as a constant responsibility and set of tasks that you must perform at the expense of your own needs. You often provide care in isolation, with little or no support.
——	**7. Usually/always over-involved:** You are supportive of your loved one, but you anxiously attend to your loved one's every need. As a result, you are devoting all your personal time to providing care, and are taking over certain aspects of your loved one's life that they, or others, could manage.

Interpreting My Score

The choice of #4 is considered *a good balance point.* This item represents the center, a place at which you find the capacity to handle your caregiving responsibilities as a manageable part of the rest of your life.

If you chose #1, #2, or #3, you are *more detached from the situation* than other caregivers. You may have some personal issues that prevent you from connecting with your loved one, performing caregiving duties or helping your caregiving partners. You and other caregivers may disagree on what kind of care, or how much care your love one needs.

If you chose #5, #6, or #7, you are *intensely involved in the caregiving role.* You may now or in the future experience depression, anxiety, or caregiver burnout. The higher your number, the greater your risk. You need to set aside more time for yourself. Find opportunities to step away from your caregiving role so you can regain a healthy balance in your life.

If your approach is causing problems for you or your caregiving partners, discuss these concerns. Identify new, more balanced ways to provide care.

Self-Care Activity #3:
Use positive thinking and self-talk

Listed below are four examples of positive messages that, with repetition, can help with relaxing and releasing the urge to control stressors which are beyond your control.

- •I can only do what I can do.
- •I let go and let God.
- •It is what it is.
- •My best is good enough.

What are difficult caregiver issues or situations over which you have no control?

Could one of these positive messages, or another of your choosing, help you conserve energy? Write this positive message in the space below.

Transfer your positive thought to a 3x5 card, a post-it note or your daily calendar. Breathe slowly and deeply as you repeat it regularly, and in specific situations when you feel out of control.

Self-Care Activity #4
Practice deep breathing to gain strength and positive energy

Try this deep breathing activity to calm yourself and reenergize. Despite the busyness of your schedule, or perhaps because of it, taking time for silence is critical to your well-being. You don't need hours, even a few minutes will help. Follow these steps:

1. Go to a quiet space where you will not be interrupted. Turn off the radio, television, computer, beeper and phone. Settle into a comfortable chair or sofa. Place your feet on the ground, or put your feet up if you like. Close your eyes.

2. Take in a deep breath from way down in your belly; fill your lungs and slowly exhale. Slowly repeat this several times and feel yourself start to relax. Continue sitting quietly, breathing deeply, rhythmically, slowly. Clear your mind of all thoughts by focusing on inhaling and exhaling. Breathe in peace and calm. Breathe out tension and pain.

3. When your mind starts wandering and thinking of other things, as it certainly will, gently refocus on inhaling and exhaling. Maintain a passive attitude; don't judge or get upset about these thoughts. Simply notice them and refocus on breathing in peace and calm; breathing out tension and pain.

4. Start by spending three minutes on this deep breathing activity and work up to twenty minutes.

5. When the time is up, gradually open your eyes and pay attention to the feeling of calm.

C4 References
*1 Adapted from:

McCleod, Beth Witrogen. Editor. *And Thou Shalt Honor: The Caregiver's Companion.* Rodale Press. 2002. Page 366.

Carmack, Betty. "Balancing engagement and detachment in caregiving." *Image.* Second Quarter, 1997. Pages 139-144.

C4 Caregiver Resources

Gawain, Shakti. *The Four Levels of Healing: A Guide to Balancing the Spiritual, Mental, Emotional and Physical Aspects of Life.* New World Library. 1997

Gawain, Shakti. *Creative Visualization.* 30th Anniversary Edition. New World Library. 2008.

Google: www.google.com Use "meditation music" to search for links to an array of free, on-line mediation music and DVD's.

McCleod, Beth Witrogen. *Caregiving: The Spiritual Journey of Love, Loss and Renewal.* John Wiley & Sons. 1999.

Miller, James. *This Time of Caregiving: Words of Encouragement and Hope.* Willowgreen 2007.

Remen, Rachel Naomi. *Kitchen Table Wisdom: Stories that Heal.* Riverhead Books. 1996.

Schaef, Anne Wilson. *Meditations for Women Who Do Too Much.* Harper Collins. 2004.

Willowgreen: www.willowgreen.com offers information, inspiration and support for life transition and aging, loss and grief, illness and caregiving, hope and spirituality, and healing presence. Samples of books and audiovisual materials that can be found at this site include:

The Art of Being a Healing Presence
The Art of Listening in a Healing Way
When you're the Caregiver/When you're Ill or Incapacitated
Change and Possibility
Finding Hope: Ways to See Life in a Brighter Light
One You Love is Dying/When You Know you're Dying
How Can I Help? /What Will Help Me? (When suffering loss)
Nothing is Permanent except Change (DVD)
Autumn Wisdom: Finding Meaning in Life's Later Years
You Shall Not Be Overcome (DVD)

⌄

....

"The real man smiles in trouble, gathers strength from distress, and grows brave by reflection."

Thomas Paine
American revolutionary leader; author of *Common Sense*

"I have just three things to teach: simplicity, patience, compassion. These three are your greatest treasures."

Lao Tzu
Chinese philosopher; founder of Taoism

"Serenity is not freedom from the storm, but peace amid the storm."

Debenport
Unknown

....

C5: Channel Your Thoughts

Jane's Story: Pennies on My Path

I am drowning! My husband is in constant pain. Dad is going blind and can hardly breathe. Mother is losing her mind. My mother-in-law had a stroke and can't care for herself anymore. I have a four-year-old son who never stops moving, and I just moved into a house that polite people would call a fixer-upper. The stress is getting to be so much that I wonder if I will lose my mind, too. My life feels like such a wreck; I'm even dreaming about debris.

Last week I dreamed I was walking on a rainy, windy night. My coat collar pulled up and my head down, I was leaning into the blustery, bitter wind. Looking down at the sodden leaves and dirt in the gutter, something caught my eye. I bent to see more clearly what it was. There in the puddle atop some muddy decaying leaves, I found a shiny penny. Into my mind popped the old saying, "Find a penny pick it up and all day long you'll have good luck." Then I noticed more coins among the rubbish in the gutter: nickels, dimes, and quarters! I felt ecstatic, and then abruptly woke. Lying in bed, for some reason I smiled and felt happy. Trash and cash in the gutter, what could this mean?

The following evening a remarkable thing happened. While

walking after dinner to clear my mind, I was deep in thought, head down, when something caught my eye. I leaned over to see what it was. There among the leaves and dirt in the road near my house was a penny! Returning home from my walk that night I smiled and felt happy like after my dream. Amazingly, in the past five days I have found four more coins in the road, and they each filled me with some inexplicable delight.

Being happy about pennies makes no logical sense, yet every time I find one I am reassured. There are many ways of interpreting my dream, but I feel as if God is talking to me through these coins, encouraging me during these tough times. He seems to be saying, "You can see me amidst the rubble in your life; just look closely and keep walking. Your life may seem to be in the gutter, but some shining moments are mixed in. I will help in ways you might overlook, because they may seem as small and insignificant as a penny. But I will provide just what you need no matter what the circumstances of your life."

Are you finding pennies on your path?

Are you walking through a difficult or dark part of life? Are you finding pennies or some other talisman as you journey on? When my life was turned upside down, I struggled to remain optimistic and find something positive among so many painful circumstances. The pennies on my path raised my spirits and helped me to see the mixture of good and bad in my life. How are you viewing your life right now? One powerful way to remain optimistic in the face of caregiving challenges is to think in positive ways...and look for some "pennies" of you own!

Self-Care Recommendations 1*

What are optimism and pessimism?

Optimism and pessimism are the lenses through which you look at the world. They color the stories you create to explain events. Whether you realize it or not, these stories are active thought patterns that you control. They become habits that determine how you respond to life events, who you become and how others respond to you. Though the facts about an event remain the same, optimistic and pessimistic stories are poles apart and create completely different realities. Whether situations are positive or negative, optimists see a glass that is at least half full, but to pessimists that same glass is half empty.

How do pessimists think?

Pessimists think positive events are unlikely to happen again, and that negative ones are likely to continue or be repeated in the future. They believe that good situations are isolated events or flukes that have nothing to do with other aspects of their lives. In contrast, they think negative circumstances are experienced in many aspects of their lives and expect that more of the same is inevitable. Finally, pessimists believe that good outcomes are brought about by others or other factors beyond their control, and the bad outcomes are usually their own fault. Pessimists emphasize the negative no matter what the facts of the situation.

How do optimists think?

Optimists think in the opposite way. They view positive events as likely to continue or be repeated in the future and negative ones as unlikely to happen again. They believe that good situations are experienced in many aspects of their lives; more of the same are inevitable. Negative experiences, on the other hand, are isolated events or flukes that have nothing to do with other aspects of their lives. Finally, optimists believe they bring about good outcomes and think the bad ones are caused by others, or by other factors beyond their control. Optimists emphasize the positive no matter what the facts of the situation.

What are the benefits of being an optimist?

If you adopt an optimistic outlook, you are likely to experience:

1. Strength to handle adversity: Optimists have the capacity to persevere and adapt in times of trouble.

2. Decreased stress: Positive thinking leads to a positive frame of mind, more success, and less stress.

3. Good physical and emotional health: Optimism is linked to positive mood and good morale in all areas of life. Optimists live longer lives...aging well, and experiencing fewer physical ills.

4. Successful relationships: People respond positively to optimists. Their view of the world is contagious and can positively influence friends and colleagues.

How can I become more optimistic?

1. Choose to change: All change starts with the decision to do something different. Any pessimistic patterns you may have will remain in place until you choose to replace these negative practices with positive ones.

2. Stop and listen to your thoughts: Pay attention. As soon as

a negative thought comes to you, replace it with a positive one. When something positive happens, stop and think more encouraging thoughts. For guidance use the ideas presented on page 74-75 in "How do optimists think?" Paint vivid and energizing images. The more you challenge negative thinking and reinforce your positive thoughts, the more automatic optimism will become.

3. Don't be a Pollyanna: Where pessimists are stopped by adverse conditions, Pollyannas are unrealistic optimists who unwisely plunge ahead, ignoring real needs or threats that can increase their stress and risk of health problems. Choose realistic optimism, a lens that promotes clear thinking. Realistic, or cautious optimists:

   - Have a positive outlook without denying reality.

   - Appreciate positive elements in a situation, while also acknowledging the negative.

   - Hope for positive outcomes without assuming good results will automatically occur.

   - Accomplish positive outcomes with hard work, planning and effective problem solving.

4. Affirm yourself: 2* Affirmations are words, brief phrases or sentences that plant optimistic images into your mind. They reprogram your mind to more optimistically see, explain and respond to situations in your life. Affirming yourself is really quite simple.

- Choose an event or behavior: a positive one to encourage, or negative one to eliminate. Choose words carefully. For a positive: Describe it as caused by you, likely to continue and affecting your entire life. For a negative: Describe it as an isolated incident, not your fault and unlikely to occur again.

- Affirm this as the reality in your life, right now. Use first-person and present tense to imagine this as a reality you are experiencing now. For example, "I am capable, confident and compassionate. I find meaning and joy in being a caregiver." Select words that are vivid, and that stir up positive feelings within. Write affirmations and post them where you will see them throughout the day.

- Regularly repeat positive affirmations silently or aloud, until you know them by heart. Savor the positive image and feelings the affirmation creates. Frequent repetition reprograms your mind.

Use Self-Care Activity #3 found on pages 82-83 to prepare affirmations for yourself.

5. Visualize: 3* Visualization is daydreaming with the positive purpose of relieving stress, overcoming obstacles, or becoming more optimistic. As a caregiver, any of these approaches may be helpful. Follow these steps and use Self-Care Activity #4, found on pages 84-86, to create a helpful visualization for yourself.

- Vividly picture a positive scene in your mind's eye like vacationing on a tropical island, completing a marathon, or experiencing a joyous birthday or holiday celebration. Use all your senses: sight, hearing, taste, touch and smell. Detail is most important. The more vivid the image, the more helpful it will be.

- Envision this as the reality in your life, right now. Create images in the first-person and present tense to picture this as a reality you are experiencing now.

- Savor that scene for several moments, several times each day. You can visualize virtually anywhere, but in bed each morning and just before sleep at night are relaxed, easy times to practice visualization. Choose a time that works best for you. Regular visualization actually creates your new reality.

6. Avoid pessimism in the world around you: Emotions are contagious. Take a break from violent images, depressing stories, and people who are downbeat. Seek out people and situations that create positive energy and reinforce positive messages for you.

7. Contain the damages: When negative events do occur, create an optimistic explanation in your mind. Think of all the extenuating circumstances that might have created the negative events. Name what outside circumstances contributed to this situation. Remember that problems in a given instance neither suggest nor confirm your personal weakness. Remind yourself that there will be many opportunities to do better in the future.

Self-Care Activities

Self-Care Activity #1: Optimist or Pessimist: Which are you?

Based on the information in the text boxes below, do you tend toward optimism or pessimism when facing adversity? Of the five items in each section, put a check next to those which most clearly describe you. What do your answers say about you? How does this affect your role as a caregiver?

	Like optimists, I tend to...
_____	Believe in my ability to make good things happen, and in the goodness of life.
_____	See opportunities. Seek out and create positive situations.
_____	See difficulty as a challenge; adapt or try harder. Persevere, patiently pursue goals and dreams.
_____	Define defeat as a temporary setback.
_____	Do better with transition, tragedy or unpredictable situations than pessimists I know.
	Like pessimists, I tend to...
_____	Have less faith in my ability to persevere and solve problems. Doubt things will ever get better.
_____	See obstacles. Take fewer risks
_____	React to stressful events with denial or avoidance.
_____	Often give up in the face of difficulties
_____	Do less well with transition, tragedy or unpredictable situations than optimists I know.

Self-Care Activity #2:
Consider these questions in self-reflection or discussions

1. Pennies are the talisman that spoke to the author of hope in times of trouble. What sign or symbol of encouragement and support am I noticing? What affect does it have on me?

2. Whether optimistic or pessimistic, life sends each of us difficulties. What differs is the response to misfortune. What are some of the caregiving difficulties that I am facing?

3. In what one caregiving situation could I practice being more optimistic? At present, what are my thoughts that are pessimistic or negative? What positive thoughts could I use to replace these?

4. A Pollyanna is an unrealistic optimist who gets into difficult situations because they unwisely plunge ahead, ignoring real needs or signs of potential problems. What fictional character or real person do I know that fits this description? Am I a Pollyanna? If so, what are some of the consequences I have suffered as a result of unrealistic optimism? How can I be more realistic about my expectations?

5. Where or when do I experience violent images, toxic behaviors, or downbeat situations? How do these impact me? What can I do to protect myself from absorbing this negativity?

Self-Care Activity #3:
What affirmation can help you overcome some caregiver stress?

Follow the four steps below to create and use a helpful affirmation in your life.

Step 1: Choose either 1 or 2 listed below, and <u>write a description of what you are trying to create</u> in your life.

1. The <u>positive</u> event, behavior, attitude or trait I want to <u>encourage</u> is...

   E.g. I want to be patient and calm when my Mother repeatedly asks the same question.

2. The <u>negative</u> event, behavior, attitude or trait I want to <u>eliminate</u> is...

   E.g. I don't want to blow up and argue when talking with my siblings about Mom's needs.

What I am trying to create:

Step 2: Using the five guidelines listed below, <u>create the affirmation</u> as if it already part of your life. Then write your affirmation in the space below.

1. Use <u>first-person</u>: Start the affirmation with "I".
2. Use <u>present-tense</u>: Select words that say it is already true, a reality you are experiencing now, not something you wish to have or hope for in the future.
3. Use <u>positive</u> words: Generate upbeat feelings within yourself.
4. Use <u>vivid</u> words: Paint a clear picture that you can see, feel, and hear.
5. Use <u>realistic</u> images: Choose hopeful, positive pictures that seem right for you.

E.g. I am patient when Mom asks the same questions over and over. Because I love her, I answer calmly and accept that she is doing the best she can.

E.g. I discuss Mom's needs calmly, respectfully and assertively. I am comfortable with the outcome of our discussion.

My affirmation is:

Step 3: Select <u>ways to remind you</u> of your affirmation.
- Regularly repeat the affirmation aloud or silently each morning when you rise, or each evening when you go to bed.
- Write your affirmation on top of your to-do list, on post-it notes or 3x5 cards that you place in prominent places.

Self-Care Activity #4:
What visualization can help you overcome some caregiver stress?

Follow the four steps below to create your own helpful visual image and use it to care for yourself.

Step 1: Choose either 1 or 2 listed below, and <u>write a description of what you are trying to create</u> in your life.

    1. Do I seek some <u>relief from the stress</u> in my life?
    E.g. In general, I feel overwhelmed by the stress in my life and just want to relax.

    2. Do I want to <u>overcome or eliminate a specific obstacle?</u>
    E.g. I don't want to blow up and argue when talking with my siblings about Mom's needs.

What I am trying to create:

Step 2: Using the four guidelines listed below; <u>envision the scene</u> as if you already have this in your life. Then, write your visualization in the space below.

    1. Use <u>first-person</u>: Picture yourself in the image.

    2. Use <u>present-tense</u>: Imagine that this picture is a reality you are experiencing right now.

    3. Use <u>positive</u> images: Generate upbeat feelings within yourself by seeing things you like and that feel good to you. The more positive, the more helpful it will be.

    4. Use <u>vivid</u> images: Paint a detailed picture using all five senses, including elements that you clearly can see, feel, taste, smell and hear. The more vivid, the more helpful it will be.

E.g. <u>To relieve stress</u>

I am lying on the beach on a tropical island. The air temperature is a warm 80 degrees; a gentle breeze is blowing in from the ocean. The warm, bright sun is sparkling off the turquoise water. I hear the waves rolling in and the sea gulls calling as they dive down and catch fish just off shore. Little shore birds are skittering up the beach just ahead of the incoming wave. Calypso music is being played on a metal drum and a trio of men is melodiously singing island songs. I am sipping a cool, refreshing pina colada, leaning back on my beach chair and wiggling my toes in the warm sand. My muscles are relaxed and I am holding my beloved's hand as we gaze on the children frolicking in the waves, squealing with delight. As I take in a deep breath I feel calm and at peace.

E.g. <u>To overcome my negative feelings and handle a difficult situation</u>

I am sitting with my brother and sister at my kitchen table. In a calm, respectful tone I ask John and Emily to visit Mom more frequently. When they begin to offer excuses why they can not do this, I inhale slowly and deeply. I feel relaxation in my chest and shoulders. I hear them accuse me of not understanding and feel a warm protective shield form around me. Their criticisms are deflected and bounce off like little rubber balls that fly off into space. They look funny and make me smile. I see myself drinking warm, sweet nectar that fills me with a sense of strength from within. I have just the right response to whatever John or Emily say. My words are assertive, respectful and calm. They listen and hear my perspective. Our discussion resolves the disagreement and Mother is well cared for.

My visualization is:

(Use another paper if you need more space.)

Step 3: Savor that scene for several moments, several times each day. You can visualize virtually anywhere, but in bed each morning and just before sleep at night are relaxed, easy times to practice visualization. Choose a time that works best for you.

✎

"It is very important to generate a good attitude, a good heart, as much as possible. From this, happiness in both the short term and long term for both yourself and others will come."

Dalai Lamah
Tibetan spiritual leader and head of state

"If you don't like something, change it. If you can't change it, change your attitude."

Maya Angelou
American writer

C5 References
1* Adapted from:
Karen Reivich and Andrew Shatte. *The Resilience Factor.* Broadway Books, New York. 2002.

2* and 3* Adapted from:
Martha Davis *et.al. The Relaxation & Stress Reduction Book.* Sixth Edition. New Harbinger, Oakland CA. 2008.

C5 Caregiver Resources

ACQYR: www.acqyr.com/category/positive-affirmation-video-reviews offers a selection of brief affirmative video presentations, sample affirmations and articles about affirmation.

Authentic Happiness:
www.authentichappiness.sas.upenn.edu offers positive psychology questionnaires and resources from The Positive Psychology Center at the University of Pennsylvania. On-line questionnaires provide feedback on character strengths and virtues, happiness, optimism, satisfaction with life, and related positive psychology topics while providing the university with confidential responses for online research studies.

Ban Breathnach, Sarah. *Simple Abundance: A Daybook of Comfort and Joy.* Time Warner. 1995.

Boargeault, Cynthia. *Centering Prayer and Inner Awakening.* Cowley Publications. 2004.

Davis, Martha *et.al. The Relaxation & Stress Reduction Book.* Sixth Edition. New Harbinger, Oakland CA. 2008.

Gawain, Shakti. *Creative Visualization.* 30th Anniversary Edition. New World Library. 2008.

Google: www.google.com Search using "visualization meditation video" to access brief on-line meditation videos.

Gratefulness: www.gratefulness.org is an international non-profit organization that provides resources for living courageously and gratefully, despite life circumstances. Their broad mission and array of resources promote reconciliation and healing for individuals, relationships and the world.

Reivich, Karen and Shatte, Andrew. *The Resilience Factor.* Broadway Books. 2002.

Tolle, Eckhart. *Stillness Speaks.* New World Library. 2003.

Spirituality and Practice: www.spiritualityandpractice.com explores the differences and commonalities between all the world's religions and spiritual paths in sections on spiritual practices, book and film reviews, DVDs, e-courses and music video play lists.

"Gratitude unlocks the fullness of life. It turns what we have into enough, and more. It turns denial into acceptance, chaos to order, confusion to clarity. It can turn a meal into a feast, a house into a home, a stranger into a friend."

Melody Beattie
Self-help author who popularized the concept of co-dependence

"The essence of optimism is that it takes no account of the present, but it is a source of inspiration, of vitality and hope where others have resigned. It enables a man to hold his head high, to claim the future for himself and not to abandon it to his enemy."

Dietrich Bonhoeffer
Theologian hanged for plot against Hitler

C6: Choose Wisely

Jane's Story: Think about your choices!

One day when my son Rob was a third grader, I went to his school for a visit. His classmates were returning from after-lunch recess, still exploding with wild energy and earsplitting "playground" voices. The din reverberated through the school hallway as Rob's teacher, Mrs. Wilson, and I came around the corner. The children didn't see either of us, but they snapped to attention when they heard Mrs. Wilson loudly clap her hands three times. Then, in a commanding, yet calm and caring tone, she called out, "Students, think about your choices and make sure they are good ones!" What a teacher!

With those few words, she transformed a pack of young ruffians into angels! The third graders quieted, formed two lines, and walked silently into their classroom. They settled into their desks and began to focus on the work at hand. If I had not seen it, I would not have believed that Mrs. Wilson's instructions could make such a difference. It was amazing!

Now, eight years later I am thinking of Mrs. Wilson's words: "Think about your choices and make sure they are good ones!" I wish those words could so easily transform my life, but I am not in the third grade. Instead of energetic playmates pushing me, it is an overwhelming list of parent-spouse-worker-caregiver responsibilities that feel like a stick poking me in the back, relentlessly driving me on. Worries about how to help both Mom and Dad from so many miles away scream out and wake me in the night. Imaginary scenarios of telling off people who bungle my parents' care are proxies for my yelling at God. How could He let Mother lose her mind and Dad lose his sight? The third graders were out of hand in a sweet, youthful way; I am out of control in a tormented way.

The kids knew what to choose to get back on track; the tone of Mrs. Wilson's voice made it completely clear. Sometimes I don't know what to choose. Move Mom to the dementia unit or keep her at home? Confront a problem or let it go? Tough it out or take the antidepressant? So much of what is happening is beyond my control: my parents' health and decline; my feelings of sadness and loss; how far away I live from my folks; how much I need to be home with my husband and yet long to be with Mom and Dad. I need to think about my choices and make sure they are healthy ones.

What kind of choices are you making?

As a caregiver you are confronted with many difficult and often painful choices. When making these caregiving choices, ask yourself the following questions about what you are choosing and how you are making your choice.

Self-Care Recommendations

Is this a healthy choice?

A wise choice is never one that undermines your health or the health of others. Health is being sound or whole, free from disease or pain in body, mind, or soul. If your choice fosters well-being in any of these areas, it likely is a very good choice.

Healthy choices also promote balance in your life. Each of us has a limited supply of resources: energy, time, patience, knowledge, money. Like an overdrawn bank account, living beyond the limits of your resources is unhealthy. So recognize your limits and make sure your choices are made with them in mind. Wise choices simplify rather than complicate your life.

Is this a loving choice?

A wise choice is never one that undermines human dignity and worth. Loving choices are made with an attitude of appreciation. They lead to caring acts that acknowledge worth, address needs, or nurture growth in you or in others. Wise caregiving choices acknowledge and respect the needs of both the caregiver and the care receiver. By caring for yourself as you care for others, you model balance and show that helping others can be a meaningful and loving choice. Wise caregiving choices send this encouraging message to all those who work with you, who witness and learn from your caregiving efforts.

Is this a "big rock"?

A wise choice is never one that loses sight of what is most vital. In Stephen Covey's work and many website postings, there is the story of a teacher standing before a group of students. Into a large clear jar are poured big rocks, then smaller pebbles to fill in the spaces. Asked if the jar is full, the class answers, "Yes." The students see they are wrong when the teacher adds sand and finally water. The restricted capacity of the jar limits how much it can hold. By starting with the big rocks the teacher fits more in than anyone could have imagined. The moral of the story: "Put the big rocks in first!"

Like the jar, you have restricted capacity; there is just so much you can take. Big rocks are the most significant things in life; things that are good for the health of your body, heart, mind and soul. Pebbles are valuable but less critical. The sand and water are fun, trivial or unnecessary aspects that may be nice but are not essential. In your life, you define what are big rocks and sand. You need self-awareness to discover the limits of your capacity, and your important values and priorities. Spending time on what is unimportant is like filling the jar with sand and water first, a poor choice because it may leave no time for what is truly vital. A wise choice is one that recognizes your limits and helps you spend time on what is most important.

Would this choice pass the "death-bed" test?

Wise choices yield outcomes that stand the test of time. When trying to make difficult choices, it is tough to maintain a clear perspective and be sure of the best choice. By focusing on a long-term perspective and on your priorities, the "death-bed" question helps you sort things out. Picture yourself lying on your death-bed, preparing to breathe your last. What would you think of your choice in that situation? Rooted in the values that are truly important to you, the "death-bed" question will help you choose wisely.

Am I letting others choose for me?

Faced with a dilemma or decision, you have no choice but to choose. You may make a decision on your own or in consultation with others. You may decide now, later, or not decide at all. Even if you opt not to make a choice, the situation unfolds. Inaction allows outside forces to select for you and create outcomes that may or may not work in your favor. When you let others choose, you run the risk of their selecting actions or outcomes that don't fit with your values, satisfy your needs or promote your well-being. Exercising choice is a powerful way to create the life you want to live. Don't give this power away to others. If you are fearful, do something to bolster your courage. Take as much time as you have; don't rush. Use both the intelligence of your mind and the understanding of your heart to help you choose wisely.

Am I being honest?

<u>About the facts</u>: Facing the facts is a key component of choosing wisely, even if you don't like the facts. Avoidance, distortion, denial and entitlement are mental tricks that deflect attention from painful realities. Face the facts.

<u>About my responsibilities</u>: The behavior you choose and decisions you make have consequences that shape your life and create your reality. Don't blame other people for difficulties in your life. Acknowledging your responsibilities and choosing wisely can sometimes demand great courage and personal strength. When you take responsibility for your life, your choices will serve you well. Take responsibility for yourself.

<u>About my viewpoint</u>: Finally, it is wise to be honest about your perspective on people and situations. Don't mistake your views for objective truth. They are not. Your perspective is just one way of interpreting reality. Others have different perspectives and they are just as valid as yours. Always check your viewpoint against real data to find the truth in a situation. Wise choices flow from an accurate grasp of reality. Acknowledge that your point of view is subjective.

Can I let go?

All of life cycles through seasons; nothing stays the same forever. When people or practices, habits or attitudes that once were life giving cease to serve your needs, holding on generates distress. Look closely to identify old patterns or relationships that undermine your well-being. It is wise to hold onto what gives meaning to your life, and to let go of relationships or routines that no longer sustain you.

Letting go can also be a choice to forgive. Forgiveness is not condoning, absolving, forgetting or self-sacrifice. It is not a clear-cut, one-time decision. Forgiveness is a process of moving beyond feelings about people or past incidents and releasing grudges, resentment or self-pity. It involves putting the past in proper perspective, and giving up the desire to punish others or yourself for past actions. Choosing to let go allows you to reclaim energy for healing and moving on to more positive life experiences.

Self-Care Activities

Self-Care Activity #1:
How do you know if this is a wise choice?

Read the questions below for help when facing hard choices.

1. **Is this a healthy choice?**
    A wise choice is never one that undermines your health or
    the health of others. It fosters well-being in body, mind and
    spirit. A healthy choice encourages judicious use of time
    and energy. Use these questions to check if your choice is
    healthy:

    •Will this simplify or complicate my life?

    •Will this throw me out of balance or promote balance in
      my life?

    •Will this help me maintain health?

    •Could this improve my health?

    •Will this overtax me and my resources?

    •If I take this on, will it help me to grow, become stron-
      ger and more capable?

Self-Care Activity #1: (Continued)
How do you know if this is a wise choice?

Read the questions below for help when facing hard choices.

2. **Is this a loving choice?**

    A wise choice is never one that undermines human dignity and worth. Loving choices lead to caring acts that acknowledge worth, address needs, or nurture growth: in yourself or in others. Use these questions to check if your choice is loving:

    - Will this reflect an attitude of respect and appreciation for me, as well as for others?

    - Will this help me maintain a loving relationship with others? Could this choice improve our relationship?

    - Will the outcomes of this choice meet the needs of my care receiver without sacrificing my own?

    - Will this choice teach a positive lesson to those who are observing?

Self-Care Activity #1: (Continued)
How do you know if this is a wise choice?

Read the questions below for help when facing hard choices.

3. **Is this a "big rock"?**
    A wise choice is never one that loses sight of what is most vital. It helps you spend time on what is of highest value to you. Judging importance is based on knowing your values and priorities. Use these questions to check if your choice honors what is truly important:

    • What gives me joy or pleasure?

    • What beliefs and values do I hold dear?

    • What talents and gifts add passion to my life?

    • What fills my life with meaning and purpose?

    • How does this choice fit with my answers to the above questions?

    • Will this choice have a huge impact on my life or the life of others? If yes, will it have a positive or negative effect?

Self-Care Activity #1: (Continued)
How do you know if this is a wise choice?

Read the questions below for help when facing hard choices.

4. **Would this choice pass the "death-bed" test?**
   Wise choices generally yield results that you feel good about. By taking a long-term perspective and focusing on your priorities, this question helps you sort things out. Use these questions to check if your choice might stand the test of time:

   • Will I respect this choice in the future?

   • Will I be proud of myself for making this choice?

   • Is it important that I make a decision right now, or can this wait awhile?

   • Is this really someone else's priority, not mine?

   • If I waited and got more information would I be more comfortable making a choice?

   • If I look back on this choice when I am breathing my last, how wise will it seem?

Self-Care Activity #1: (Continued)
How do you know if this is a wise choice?

Read the questions below for help when facing hard choices.

5. **Am I letting others choose for me?**
    When you let others choose, you run the risk of their making decisions that don't fit with your values, satisfy your needs or promote your well-being. Use these questions to see if you are being passive or avoiding a decision:

    • Am I backing away from this choice out of worry or fear?

    • Am I letting others discuss this choice, while I remain silent or uninvolved?

    • Am I gathering information I need to help me make a wise choice?

    • Do I have a history of going along with others' decisions and not thinking for myself?

    • What could happen if I let others make this choice without my input?

    • What gain, benefit or satisfaction do I receive by letting others make the choice?

    • What positive benefit would be gained if I were to actively engage in making this choice?

Self-Care Activity #1: (Continued)
How do you know if this is a wise choice?

Read the questions below for help when facing hard choices.

6. **Am I being honest with myself?**
   Making wise choices requires honesty, at three levels:
   1) facing the facts of a situation, even if you don't like them;
   2) taking responsibility for your behavior, decisions and their
   consequences; and 3) accepting that your perspectives are
   subjective, and may be wrong. Use these questions to check if
   you are looking at things realistically:

   • Are there some facts that I don't want to face?

   • Is there something painful in a situation that I'm trying
     to avoid?

   • Am I ignoring what others are trying to make me see?

   • Am I blaming others for something that is really my fault
     or responsibility?

   • Are there times when I close my mind to ideas or perspec-
     tives that differ from mine?

   • Am I open to changing my views on a situation I'd rather
     not face?

   • If others view this situation differently than I do, what
     part of their perspective is useful?

Self-Care Activity #1: (Continued)
How do you know if this is a wise choice?

Read the questions below for help when facing hard choices.

7. **If it is called for, am I letting go?**
   It is wise to hold onto what gives energy and meaning to your life. It is wise to let go when what you do, how you do it, or who you're hanging out with no longer sustains you. Use these questions to see if you are holding on when you shouldn't:

   • To what am I holding on, and what is the cost of that choice?

   • What gain, benefit or satisfaction do I receive by holding on?

   • What positive benefit would be gained if I let go of this practice, relationship or attitude?

   • What could I do to help release my grasp on that which I need to let go?

   • Who could help me let go?

Self-Care Activity #2:
Consider these questions in self-reflection or discussions

1. As a caregiver, what are my biggest decisions or most difficult choices? What makes them so big or difficult?

2. What is the best caregiving decision I ever made? What made it so? Is there a lesson I learned that could be applied to future choices?

3. What is the biggest mistake I made when making a caregiving decision or choice? What made it so? Is there a lesson I learned that could be applied to future choices?

4. Who are people on whom I can rely when faced with difficult choices in each of these areas:

• Health care:

• Insurance:

• Finances:

• Legal matters:

• Household management:

• Handling emotions:

• Are there other areas where I need help with making choices, and to whom can I turn for help?

5. What are some healthy choices I have made for myself? How did these affect my family or friends? Would I make the same choices in the future? If so, why? If not, why not?

6. What are some of the unhealthy choices I make? What are the results associated with my unhealthy choices, the consequences for me or for others?

7. Are there times when I avoid choosing or let others choose for me? What are the results, either positive or negative, that are associated with "choosing not to choose?"

8. What are the "big rocks" in my life, the values and priorities I need to honor when I make choices?

9. When being honest about my caregiving situation is difficult, what are the facts I would rather avoid, deny or change? What are my responsibilities that I'd rather not have to do? Which of my personal perspectives do I treat as if they were objective fact? What are the consequences of being less than honest with myself?

Self-Care Activity #3: Reflect on letting go

Read the following poem to help you reflect on your feelings about letting go of situations that no longer give energy, joy, purpose or meaning to your life.

To "Let Go" Takes Love
(Author Unknown)

To "Let Go" does not mean to stop caring.
It means I can't do it for someone else.

To "Let Go" is not to enable,
but to allow learning from natural consequences.

To "Let Go" is to admit powerlessness,
which means the outcome is not in my hands.

To "Let Go" is not to care for, but to care about.

To "Let Go" is not to fix, but to be supportive.

To "Let Go" is not to judge,
but to allow another to be himself or herself.

To "Let Go" is not to be in the middle arranging all the outcomes,
but to allow others to determine their own destinies.

To "Let Go" is not to be less protective,
it is to permit another to face reality.

To "Let Go" is not to dominate,
but to be willing to let things happen.

To "Let Go" is to not to betray the past,
but to have faith in the future.

To "Let Go" means to fear less and to love more.

Reflection questions:

- What responsibilities, people, thought patterns, behaviors, habits, or living arrangements do you need to let go?

- How are you handling these situations?

- How do you feel about letting go?

- Do you need some help? Who could you go to for help?

- What action on your part would help you to let go?

- What benefits might you receive if you let go?

....

"Forgiveness does not change the past but it does enlarge the future."

Paul Boese

Dutch botanist, known for famous quotes

"Realize deeply that the present moment is all you ever have. Make the Now the primary focus of your life."

Eckhart Tolle

Spiritual teacher and author of *The Power of Now*

....

C6 Caregiver Resources

Bridges, William and Susan. *Managing Transitions: Making the Most of Change.* Third Edition. DaCapo Press. 2009.

Bridges, William. *Transitions: Making Sense of Life's Changes.* DaCapo Press. 2004.

Covey, Stephen. *The 7 Habits of Highly Effective People.* Fireside Books. 1989.

Douty, Linda. *How Can I Let Go if I Don't Know I'm Holding On?* Morehouse Publishing. 2005.

Fear of Transformation: a brief, inspirational story about change and transition, can be accessed on the web at: **http://www.inspirationalarchive.com/texts/topics/transformation/feartran.shtml** This story is taken from *The Essene Book of Days* by Danaan Parry.

Miller, James. *Welcoming Change: Discovering Hope in Life's Transitions.* Augsburg Fortress. 1997.

Peck, M. Scott. *The Road Less Traveled.*, Simon and Schuster. 1978.

Campaign for Love & Forgiveness: **www.loveandforgive.org** is a project of the Fetzer Institute, a community engagement initiative that encourages people to bring love and forgiveness into the heart of individual and community life.

Tolle, Eckhart. *A New Earth: Awakening to Your Life's Purpose.* Penguin Group. 2005.

C7: Cultivate Community

Jane's Story: Why won't you walk with me?

I don't understand why some of my closest friends and family seem to be AWOL: absent without leave during these desperate days. Maybe they don't recognize my desperation. Dad unexpectedly died within hours of having a stroke 10 months ago, on Mother's Day. Mom's dementia has gotten much worse since then. A small group of steadfast souls still see Mom since Dad's death, but most have stopped visiting. Few call to offer support, and some don't even ask how things are going. Maybe they don't want to know.

Why am I so angry? Everyone is busy. People may not know what to say. Some family members have been distant for years. I shouldn't expect anything different now, but I guess I do. I want family and friends I can depend on for support. I long for relationships that feel life giving like oxygen.

I am really hurt, as well as angry. I feel let down. I would like to be able to turn to others for help to get through these horrors called dementia and death. Sometimes, when there is no specific task that can be done, I simply could use a hug from a loving person. In times of crisis isn't it natural to turn to our family and friends for support? Don't I have a right to be disappointed and mad?

Do you ever feel disconnected from the support of family or friends?

Although I had a right to feel disappointed and mad, it was a huge waste of time and energy. It took buckets of tears and more than a year's time after my Mother's death to see that I was looking for help where it could not be found. For many reasons, some of my friends and family were not there for me when I really needed them.

How about you? Are you in dire need of support? Do you have a circle of family and friends who are there for you in times of need? The caregiving experience showed me the importance of cultivating a diverse community who would sustain me when life is difficult. It taught me that clinging to my wants and expectations, and asking "Why?" causes problems. I learned another lesson the hard way. Asking for help from someone who hasn't got it to give is as futile as trying to find milk in an egg carton.

Self-Care Recommendations

Why is connecting with others so important?

As a human being, you are a social animal, wired for relating to other people. You gain strength and energy from connecting with your spouse or other family members; with friends, neighbors or people in your faith community. The positive benefits that come from cultivating a supportive community include:

1. Improved health: Encouragement and assistance from oth-

ers reduces stress and helps you cope. It strengthens your resilience and immune system, and helps preserve your health.

2. Richer resources: No one person has all of the skills, talents, knowledge, assets or energy to "do it all." Connecting with others gives you access to information, resources and capable people that can help you.

3. Smarter choices: Complicated, life-altering decisions can become clear when others share their ideas. Your support system can also reassure you when decisions are difficult.

4. Better balance: Your energy for juggling life responsibilities is finite, yet as a caregiver, your list of tasks at times seems endless. Turning over some tasks to others cuts overload and helps keep your life in balance.

5. Deeper appreciation: Caring for your loved one can be both awful and amazing. On one hand, you face difficult decisions, duties and exhausting responsibilities. On the other hand, helping is an act of love, an honor and one of the most profound experiences that life has to offer. Connecting with others helps you live with the dilemmas, understand the paradoxes, and appreciate the beauty of being a caregiver.

What can I do to connect with others?

Share Your Caregiving Story
As a caregiver your life is filled with experiences that are sad,

miraculous, humbling, tragic, frightening, puzzling, infuriating, inspiring, hilarious and often mundane. These deeply personal and powerful experiences make up your caregiving story. Like scenes in a movie or chapters in a book, your story unfolds as you journey through caregiving with your loved ones and friends. But what do you do with that story?

In the hectic life of a caregiver, you race along, accomplishing so much, but often doing it in isolation and under incredible stress. For some energy, encouragement, relief and fun, try connecting with others by sharing your stories. Discuss your serious concerns and problems, ponder the meaning and importance of being a caregiver, but also tell tales of funny, ironic or unbelievable situations. Talking about your experiences and emotions is not an idle way of just passing time; it is a means of both getting and giving the support that is critical to continuing in your caregiving role. Storytelling can be revitalizing, inspiring and fun. And it is easy; sharing your stories requires no equipment, supplies, or training. It doesn't cost a dime or take much time, but there is usually a huge payback in exchanging experiences with others. Through the simple yet powerful exchange of stories, you can connect and be refreshed by the caring of others.

Storytelling is not just for children. Here are situations where the exchange of stories could give you the strength and support you need to carry on:

- Reminisce with one who is elderly or terminally ill. Consider recording these reminiscences for posterity.
- Participate in a support group, class or discussion group.

- Talk with a counselor or clergy person about difficulties you face with your caregiving role.
- Listen as your care receiver or other caregivers retell stories of life-changing or traumatic incidents.
- Recount a true personal story, or fictional fable to teach others what you have learned in your experience.
- Relate old family stories to teach young family members about what important values define your family and support you in being a caregiver.
- Converse on the phone or at a meal with family and friends, for no other reason than to receive their understanding, encouragement, and comfort.
- Record your family caregiving experiences in journal, essay, poem, prose or dramatic formats.
- Ask other family caregivers to tell about their experiences as caregivers.
- Read inspiring stories from literature, religious texts, or caregiver publications.
- Watch movies which depict the challenges and importance of caring for others.

Feast on relationships with family and friends

Picture the community around you as a well-stocked refrigerator that is filled with food to sustain you. Healthy caregivers strike a balance between doing their work and preserving their capacity to care. Energy flows out when providing care; that energy needs to be replenished. Sustenance to refuel your body and soul can be found in the community of family and friends who surround you.

1. <u>Open the door</u>: Like a well-stocked refrigerator in the heart of your home, the refreshment you so need to continue car-

ing is there for you, if you just open the door. Go to your friends and family to be fed.

2. <u>Feast on healthy food, as well as on a few treats</u>. Think about what you need, what would relieve your stress or solve some of your caregiving problems. Also think of your wants; what would simply be fun and pleasing to do with a friend or family member. In life as in caregiving, sometimes we need a full meal; sometimes we just want a cookie. Look to your friends and family for both.

3. <u>Feed yourself—ask for what you need.</u> When your body needs food you don't wait for others to guess if you are hungry. You don't criticize yourself for being hungry. You open the refrigerator door and get some food. So as a caregiver, don't passively wait for others to guess your needs, or apologize for having needs. Ask others to help with any of your caregiving tasks. Also, ask for help managing your own affairs that, because of caregiving responsibilities have become too much to handle. Be specific, direct and respectful when you ask for help.

4. <u>Let others feed you</u>. Don't always try to do things yourself. Take in energy from the community of friends and family who support you; allow them to feed you. If accepting help is difficult for you, remember that it feels good to give. In receiving, you offer others an opportunity to affirm their generosity and express their love. Graciously accept help that is offered, in whatever form it takes.

5. <u>Choose dependable brands</u>. Your support system is like the

contents of your refrigerator; some brands and some people deliver the goods better than others. Go to reliable supporters who are concerned about you; optimistic and hopeful, yet realistic people who can listen and help you make good decisions. Avoid negative or self-centered people who make you feel guilty or uncomfortable for needing help.

6. <u>Look for milk in the milk carton, not in the egg carton.</u> You know it is absurd to look for milk among the eggs. Don't waste your energy seeking help from people who are unable or unwilling to provide what you need. Seek support from those who want to support you. Also, ask others to do things that they like, that they are good at, or feel comfortable doing. This approach increases the likelihood of actually receiving the help you need, and allows those who give to feel good about doing something for you.

7. <u>Go to the pitcher that is full, not the one that's empty.</u> Seeking support from folks who are tapped out or over committed is as unsatisfying as trying to get a glass of juice from an empty pitcher. Look for help from people who have a bit more time or balance in their lives. Also, don't be too quick to judge those who are over extended. They have a right to choose how they spend their time; you do not own their lives…they do. Accept the reality of others' limitations. Empty pitchers are empty. Being upset won't fill them up.

8. <u>Restock the refrigerator.</u> Just as the refrigerator runs low on food without a replenishing trip to the market, relationships with those in your support system get depleted without your giving something back. Tending relationships

and recognizing people refills the reservoir of good will that energizes your supporters to help during difficult times. How do you restock? Here are some ideas you might find helpful:

- Express gratitude. Say "thank you" in person, by phone, email or writing a note of thanks.
- Demonstrate genuine interest. Ask about what is happening in the other's life; listen to their response.
- Show kindness and respect. Speak and act in ways that show you care. Treat others as you would like to be treated.
- Keep commitments. Follow through and do what you say you will do. Be realistic about your energy and time; do not offer to do what you are unable to do.
- Sincerely apologize when you have done something to hurt or offend.

....

"Solitude vivifies; isolation kills."

Joseph Roux
French cartographer

"If we don't give kindness to ourselves and accept support from others, then we risk becoming disenchanted with the caregiving role when we could be blessed by it instead. Even the Lone Ranger relied on Tonto."

Beth Witrogen McCleod
Writer, speaker and consultant on caregiving issues

....

Self-Care Activities

Self-Care Activity #1:
Consider these questions in self-reflection or discussions

1. Do I "open the door" to support from others, or tend to handle caregiving concerns on my own? What positive benefits do I get from my usual approach? What are the costs associated with not opening the door to others' support?

2. Who are my "dependable brands", those friends and family who are reliable, realistic and really helpful people? Have I told them lately how much their support means? Offering recognition and thanks costs nothing but is an invaluable gift to the receiver. It is a sure way to keep relationships open and strong.

3. When have I looked for "milk in an egg carton", seeking support from someone unable or unwilling to provide what I needed? What was the outcome of that situation: did I get the help I requested? How comfortable did it feel? If the situation did not work well, is there another source I could turn to if I need that type of help in the future?

4. Are there "empty pitchers" in my community of support, people who are tired, over-committed, or out of balance in their own lives? Are there other sources I can turn to instead of these people? How do I feel when an "empty pitcher" lets me down? When angry or upset, I need to work in my own heart to let go of judgment and negative feelings. No matter how justified, holding onto these emotions will hurt me and drain away energy.

5. What difficulties and challenges are my supportive friends and family facing? Have I asked them recently about their concerns and listened with interest and empathy? Being realistic about my own energy, how could I extend myself to them in some meaningful way?

6. The four categories of caregiving help are described in Self-Care Activity #4 on pages 124-125. Which of these ways of helping are easiest for me? Which are most difficult or uncomfortable? Which are impossible for me to do? Who are my partners with skills to complement mine, and do they offer them? If not, who could I ask for help doing those necessary things that I can't, or don't feel able to do?

Self-Care Activity #2:
Are you T-I-R-E-D and in need of help?

If someone offered to help you right now how would you respond? Be ready to take advantage of such an offer by making a "Help Wanted List" *1 on a sheet of paper, your hand-held planning device, several 3x5 cards or post-it notes that you carry in your wallet, calendar or purse. Use the acronym "TIRED" to help construct your list. Refer to it when someone with a kind heart offers to help you. And if no one is offering, hire some help if you can afford to, or ask those kind hearted friends if they will help. They just might say yes!

Tasks

I need someone to help with these day-to-day tasks: the physical care my loved one needs, yard or household chores, errands or transportation, personal finances, plant, pet or child care. Who could fill this need?

Information

I need help in finding out about my loved one's condition, treatment, and prognosis, as well as the knowledge or skills I need to be an effective caregiver. Who could fill this need?

Respite

I need someone to help me get a break for a few moments, for several hours on a given date, for one or several days off-duty or for an extended vacation. Who could fill this need?

Emotional support

I need someone to be present to me and ask how I am doing, to listen to me with empathy, understanding and without judgment. Who could fill this need?

Decision making

I need someone to help me decide how to handle a situation, solve a problem, or navigate the health care, legal or insurance system. Who could fill this need?

Self-Care Activity #3:
Who are your partners on the path?

Caregivers usually have partners who share in the caring: family members, friends or people from other communities. With a cooperative team, helping a loved one becomes easier, and sometimes a joy. But when a caregiver is totally alone or when relationships among caregivers break down, helping becomes difficult. Use this chart to assess your caregiving partnerships. The wider and more helpful your network, the more strength you will have for caring.

Circle the number in the box that describes the quality of support you receive from these parties. I get cooperative support and effective help from:	Never, or Does not apply to me	Very Rarely	With some regularity	Very often	Constantly
1. My spouse	0	1	2	3	4
2. My child/children	0	1	2	3	4
3. My sibling(s)/brother- or sister-in-law	0	1	2	3	4
4, My parent(s)	0	1	2	3	4
5. My aunt(s)/uncle(s)	0	1	2	3	4
6. My niece(s)/nephew(s)	0	1	2	3	4
7. My cousin(s)	0	1	2	3	4
8. My grandchild/children	0	1	2	3	4
9. My grandparent(s)	0	1	2	3	4
10. My neighbor(s)	0	1	2	3	4
11. My friend(s)	0	1	2	3	4
12. Members of my faith community	0	1	2	3	4
13. Members of my support group	0	1	2	3	4
14. Members of my online community	0	1	2	3	4
15. Professionals who help me and/or my loved one	0	1	2	3	4
To tally your score, add the numbers circled in each column, and then add the numbers across this row. My total score is:_____					

Interpreting My Score

These items provide a <u>snapshot of your support network</u>, the help you have for being a caregiver.

The maximum <u>score of 60</u> is unlikely; most people find that some categories do not apply to them.

<u>Total scores of 0-29</u>, as well as <u>a response of 0 or 1 to most items</u> suggest *minimal, intermittent or poor quality support.* This puts you at risk for feeling alone and overburdened, for becoming overly reliant on a few people, and for becoming ill or burning out. Protect yourself by actively expanding the size of your network and quality of support you receive. Open up; share your needs and feelings on a deeper level. Reach out to new people. Join online or in-person support groups. Use suggestions from the section titled, "What can I do to connect with others?" found on pages 111-116, to help cultivate your community of support.

<u>Total scores of 30 and above</u>, as well as <u>responses of 3 or 4</u> on many items, indicates a *large and strong network.* Continue linking to these people to retain your health, well-being and capacity to care.

Self-Care Activity #4:
How does each of you contribute to caring? *2

Caregivers are helpful in many ways. Different people help in different ways, based on their strengths and the other responsibilities in their lives. No one person can provide all types of care.

Put a check next to each of the ways you help. Ask your caregiving partners to complete this form, also. Compare your answers; discuss what you need to do to cooperate and fairly share caregiving responsibilities.

1. **Providing Physical Care**

___ **Feeding**: Assisting with eating meals

___ **Bathing**: Assisting with bath or shower; getting into and out of tub/shower

___ **Dressing**: Dressing and choosing appropriate clothing

___ **Toileting**: Getting to and using the toilet

___ **Grooming**: Combing hair, cleaning teeth/dentures, caring for glasses, finger/ toe nails

___ **Mobility**: Support when walking; helping with stairs, escalators, or revolving doors

2. **Managing Household Affairs**

___ **Meals**: Preparing/arranging for meals; managing food supplies

___ **Housekeeping**: Keeping neatness and cleanliness in the home

___ **Shopping**: Purchasing groceries/clothing/personal items; accompanying on shopping trips

___ **Laundry**: Washing or dry-cleaning; taking care of clothing

___ **Home Maintenance**: Repairing; keeping home/yard in good condition; emptying trash; shoveling/mowing

___ **Realty and Relocation**: Organizing home sales/purchases and move to new living arrangement

3. Managing Personal Affairs

___ <u>Medications</u>: Buying, giving medication; offering reminders of medication times; monitoring drug safety

___ <u>Substance Abuse</u>: Addressing problems with drinking or misuse of other medications

___ <u>Safety</u>: Reminding to lock doors, turn off oven, fasten seat belt; rescinding driver's license

___ <u>Transportation</u>: Driving/arranging for transportation; maintaining car; acting as a travel companion

___ <u>Finances</u>: Managing banking and bills, assets and investments; balancing checkbook; preparing taxes

___ <u>Legal services</u>: Managing legal issues and documents; assuming power of attorney

___ <u>Insurance</u>: Handling private insurance, Medicare/Medicaid, Social Security, VA or other benefits

___ <u>Care Coordination</u>: Communicating with professionals or organizations providing health/elder care; accompanying to medical appointments, tests or procedures

___ <u>Technology Support</u>: Helping with phone, email, computer, TV, electrical or mechanical equipment

4. Providing Emotional and Social Support

___ <u>Communication</u>: Helping to speak, read, write, or comprehend what others are communicating

___ <u>Mental Function</u>: Reminding about appointments, directions, names, events; guiding decisions

___ <u>Mood</u>: Boosting outlook on life and self-esteem; supporting through grief or stress; listening

___ <u>Behavior</u>: Encouraging a usual pattern of activity or cueing socially-acceptable behavior

___ <u>Social life</u>: Arranging or transporting to social engagements with family and friends

___ <u>Presence</u>: Calling, visiting or writing; sharing feelings/thoughts; encouraging contact with others

Self-Care Activity #5:
How do you each handle your caregiver role?

Being a caregiver is a role, a set of tasks and expectations that you take on, sometimes voluntarily, sometimes not. Like an actress or actor playing a role, different people approach caregiving from different perspectives. No two caregivers fill this role in exactly the same way. No one style is best. It helps you, the person you are helping, and your caregiving partners if you recognize and work out your different approaches.

To assess your caregiving style, read the two different approaches described in each of the eight boxes below. Put an "X" at the place on the continuum that best describes you. Ask your caregiving partners to complete this form, also. Compare your answers. Discuss the similarities and differences in your approaches; how these lead to cooperation or conflicts among you. Identify ways to foster better understanding and cooperation among you.

1. My general approach to caregiving responsibilities

I like to organize and make plans.   I like to be flexible and go with the flow.

X---X

2. My level of involvement in caregiving responsibilities

I am on the sidelines and let others lead.   I am in the thick of things, doing lots to help.

X---X

3. My general outlook on caregiving

I am pessimistic; there are always problems.   I am optimistic; things will be fine.

X---X

4. Ways I learn what I need to know about caregiving

I methodically gather information; focus on details and facts.   I focus on the big-picture; get details only when needed.

X---X

5. Ways I make decisions about caregiving

I weigh pros and cons and emphasize logic.   I trust my feelings and go with my gut.

X---X

6. Ways I maintain my energy for caregiving

I need people and activities to reenergize.   I need quiet and solitude to reenergize.

X---X

7. Ways I react to disagreements or difficult caregiving situations

I keep my thoughts to myself, avoid or withdraw.   I show strength, exert control, or get aggressive.

X---X

8. My general outlook on the change that comes with caregiving.

I feel loss; am sad, angry, anxious, numb or unsure.   I recognize the change, but feel fine and want to move on.

X---X

C7 References
*1 Adapted from:
Elizabeth Eby. *Help! I Need Somebody.* http://www.strengthfor-caring.com Accessed October 14, 2009.

*2 Adapted from:
Beth Witrogen McLeod, Editor. *And Thou Shalt Honor: The Caregiver's Companion.* Rodale Press. Pages 30-32.
Based on work of The Pennsylvania State University Gerontology Center. University Park, PA.

C7 Caregiver Resources
Capossela, Cappy and Warnock, Sheila. *Share the Care: How to Organize a Group to Care for Someone Who Is Seriously Ill.* Fireside. Second Edition 2004.

Disease-Specific Sites such as:
Alzheimer's Type Dementia – www.alz.org
Arthritis – www.arthritis.org
Blindness – www.blindness.org
Cancer – www.cancer.org and www.cancercare.org
Diabetes – www.diabetes.org
Heart disease – www.americanheart.org
Huntington's Disease – www.hdsa.org
Kidney – www.kidneyfund.org
Liver – www.liverfoundation.org
Lung – www.lungusa.org
Mental Illness – www.nmha.org
Neuromuscular – www.alsa.org and www.mda.org
Multiple Sclerosis – www.nmss.org
Osteoporosis – www.nof.org

Pain – www.painfoundation.org and
www.partnersaginstpain.com
Parkinson Disease – www.apdparkinson.com
Spinal Cord Injury – www.spinalcord.org
Stroke – www.stroke.org

Eldercare Locator: www.eldercare.gov/Eldercare.net/Public/ Home.asp connects older Americans and their caregivers with sources of information on local service providers throughout the country. The service links those who need assistance with state and local area agencies on aging and community-based organizations that serve older adults and their caregivers. Call the Eldercare Locator toll-free at 1-800-677-1116.

Maguire, Jack. *The Power of Personal Storytelling.* Penguin Putnam. 1998.

Meade, Erica. *Tell It By Heart: Women and the Healing Power of Story.* Dreamcatcher/Open Court. 1995.

National Association of Geriatric Care Managers: www. caremanager.org supports its members, and helps the general public learn about and connect with professionals who can help coordinate eldercare.

Owens, Virginia. *Caring for Mother: A Daughter's Long Goodbye.* Westminster John Knox Press. 2007.

Rooks, Diane. *Spinning Gold out of Straw: How Stories Heal.* Salt Run Press. 2001.

Share the Caregiving: www.sharethecare.org educates the public, health professionals and clergy about group caregiving as a proven option for meeting the needs of the seriously ill or dying, those in rehabilitation, the elderly in need of assistance and their caregivers.

Stone, Richard. *The Healing Art of Storytelling.* Hyperion. 1996.

Well Spouse Association: www.wellspouse.org is a national, not-for-profit membership organization which gives support to wives, husbands, and partners of the chronically ill and/or disabled by offering support groups, a quarterly newsletter, online mentors and respite weekends.

"Condemn none: if you can stretch out a helping hand, do so. If you cannot, fold your hands, bless your brothers, and let them go their own way."

Swami Vivekananda
Indian leader and Hindu teacher

"A small body of determined spirits fired by an unquenchable faith in their mission can alter the face of history."

Mohandas Gandhi
Indian leader; advocate of non-violent protest

"If we have no peace, it is because we have forgotten that we belong to each other."

Mother Theresa
Roman Catholic nun and humanitarian

Made in the USA
Middletown, DE
10 November 2017